EVERYONE ELSE'S CHILDREN

Linda Sawley

To Sharon.
Bet you never thought
you'd end up in a book!
Enjoy!
Linda Sawley (or Miss Linda!)
May 2003.

**LINRIC PUBLISHING
ENGLAND**

Published in 1998 by LinRic Publishing
18, Victoria Lodge
Read, Lancs, BB12 7SZ

British Library Cataloguing in Publication Data
Sawley, Linda
TITLE - Everyone Else's Children
I. Title
Classification   B/SAW
ISBN number 0 9534329 0 4

Perfect Bound in Great Britain by the University of Central
Lancashire, Preston, Lancs, PR1 2HE.

<u>DEDICATION</u>

Dedicated to my Mum who
sadly died during the writing of this book.
She would have been so proud.

Acknowledgements

Richard I'Anson - my computer expert, Kim Chappell - Typist, Norma, David and Janet at the University of Central Lancashire Printing Services, Kathleen Bulcock of Burnley Writers' Circle, Sarah Stott - Yorkshire Art Circus, Caroline Collins and Louise at the Royal College of Nursing, Vicky Webster.

To all the patients and colleagues who have inspired this book and made my life richer and without whom I could not have written this book.

The names of patients and staff in this book have been omitted to avoid any breach of staff or patient confidentiality.

CHAPTER ONE

<u>BORN AWKWARD</u>

"Born awkward," my Dad always used to say, "and been awkward ever since!" I suppose there was some justification. I was the second daughter of Mum and Dad, Jean and Donald. My sister Cynthia had been born two years previously. In the forties, you could claim an Income Tax rebate for the whole of the previous year up to the 5th of April. Dad missed his windfall twice. Cynthia was born on the 9th April 1947, even though she was due at the end of March. They tried to avoid this happening with me. Despite the fact that I was due in the middle of March, I was even lazier. On the 5th of April, I still had not put in an appearance. Dad took Mum out for a ride in the car, up hills, down dales, and over cobblestone streets. All to no avail. I arrived on the 6th April, and once again Dad missed his rebate. Hence the accusation that I was born awkward.

Not only had I lost him money at birth, he was forking out money ever after for me. It certainly did not stop at my birth. After their marriage, my parents had lived with Mum's parents until they found a house of their own. They found a dinky little two bedroomed bungalow, which was far too small once I arrived. The move to the new house took place when I was six months old, and we moved into a very large terraced house in a pleasant residential area. Apart from the long terrace where we lived, the rest of the avenue was semi-detached houses, built in the late thirties. Dad's parents, Granny and Grampa Clarkson, lived in one of the semis, across the road from us, which had both disadvantages as well as advantages. We stayed there until just after my fourth birthday, and once again it was my fault that we had to move.

Cynthia had been going to an excellent primary school called Rosehill and was doing very well there. My parents obviously wanted me to go to the same school, but because the school was becoming very popular, they had tightened the intake boundaries, and yes, you've guessed it, we were outside the boundary, and we had to move house again so that I could go to the same school.

I have only a few memories of those first four years. I can remember the kitchen, lounge, hall and garden at that house, but I cannot remember the rest of the house. My earliest memory was at two years old. My uncle and aunty contracted tuberculosis (T.B.) and had to be admitted to hospital. My cousin Colin who was the same age as Cynthia, moved in with us for six months. As a precaution, Mum had myself and Cynthia X-rayed and vaccinated. I remember going to the X-ray department, the waiting room and the equipment. Strangely, I don't remember the injection or the fact that Colin lived with us. Cynthia does because she says that Colin was always bullying her!

Other memories include playing in the long back garden, or on spare land at the back of the house. One Bonfire Night a firework exploded in a neighbour's face, and I remember Mum going into the neighbour's house several times a day to put eye drops in. Another memory is of Mum hiding the biscuit tin on a high cupboard so that we could not reach it. But Cynthia and I soon worked out a system to get at the biscuits. We put a stool onto a chair, to climb onto the work surface, to reach the top of the cupboard. Nothing would keep us from the biscuits! It is probably those early struggles and ingenuity to get to the biscuits that is responsible for our life-long weight problems. This was also helped by the fact that we lived so near Granny. She always had a plentiful supply of sweets, chocolates, and delicious tasting sarsaparilla and dandelion and burdock pop in stone flagons. Granny was very indulgent both to herself and us!

My fourth birthday also stands out as a milestone in my early memory. At the end of the party Dad arrived home with a new car. It was black, as most of them were in those days, and was an Austin A90. We loved it immediately and called it Topsy. The highlight of the party was that Dad piled us all into the car and took us for a drive. Not many of our friends had a car so it was a great novelty all round. We probably would not have been able to afford a car but Grampa Clarkson's eyesight was failing, and he bought the car for Dad. It was a very good arrangement for us. Grampa bought the car, paid for all the petrol, servicing and repairs, and even paid Dad for garaging and cleaning the car. All Dad had to do was drive it! But there were strings attached. Each Saturday Dad had to take Granny out for a drive to the sea-side, or wherever else she wanted to go, and he had to take them to church on Sundays.

Dad's other duty as a chauffeur was to take Grampa to the bus-stop every morning, so that he could catch the Manchester bus to work. The family owned a cotton mill called Sutcliffe and Clarkson. It had been started by Grampa's Mum and her brother, Jimmy Sutcliffe. They were both cotton weavers, and when they inherited a little money, they decided that they would open their own weaving shed in 1911. Strangely enough Grampa's Mum ran the business with her brother, whilst her husband worked in the mill. This was very unusual for the era, but she had far more business sense than her husband. Her brother Jimmy was a well-known character in the town, and became a town councillor. My claim to fame is that he was the Mayor of Burnley (on two consecutive occasions) in the twenties. His picture used to be in the local museum and stately home, Towneley Hall. I used to drag my friends there to look at his picture.

Great-grandma Clarkson had twelve children, but only half of them survived to adult life which was quite common in those days. She was in her late forties when she had her last child, Lizzie, but would not give up going to work at the mill. The eldest daughter, Mary, had to stay at home and look after her. As the children grew up, two of the surviving boys went to work in the offices of the mill. John stayed in the offices, but eventually Grampa became the 'Manchester Man.' All the local cotton mills had a Manchester Man. He would go each day to Manchester to the cotton exchange (now the Royal Exchange Theatre) to sell the cotton woven at the mill in Burnley. Grampa had the reputation of being the quickest man on 'Change, as the cotton exchange was called. Most Manchester Men had an office nearby. After the days work they would go back to their office and work out a price for the orders of cotton. The next day they would go back with the price, to clinch the deal. Grampa was very quick at mental arithmetic and could work the price out in his head, and could give a quote the same day. Hence he got the business and the reputation to go with it. Unfortunately I did not inherit Grampa's mathematical ability, more the reverse! In the second year of secondary school, I was put in the A group, but I was quickly demoted to the B group, then to C, then to D. Eventually I was put in the remedial class for those who were too thick to do 'O' level. But I am digressing (a thing I do frequently I hear my friends saying)!

Back to the mill. As years went by, my Dad and his two cousins joined the mill. Dad was the export manager, and a rare treat for us was to go down to the mill with Dad, where we got thoroughly spoilt by all and sundry. An even rarer and far better treat was to go to Manchester with Grampa. As the cotton trade dwindled in Lancashire, the business on the 'Change dwindled as well, but Grampa still attended every day until it closed in about 1969. He was by then in his seventies, and did not retire until the business was sold in 1975, when he was 78. A day at Manchester was very leisurely by the late sixties. It usually meant catching the 8.30 am bus from Burnley. On arrival in

Manchester, the first stop was the Kardomah cafe for coffee, a cigarette and a gossip with his cronies. Then he would let us loose in Manchester with some spending money, whilst he went on the 'Change. We met up again at lunch-time.

Lunch was always eaten at Kendal's, at the top floor restaurant, where Grampa had his own personal waitress called Lucy - a lovely lady. A little more shopping after lunch, whilst Grampa went to the 'Change again or to his office. Then it was back to Kardomah's for a cup of tea before boarding the bus back home to Burnley. What a thrill to be treated as a grown up, by going to work with Grampa. What a shame that the 'Change closed. I could have enjoyed a job like that, dossing around in Manchester whilst working for the family firm, but I suppose I would have needed a calculator!

Whilst Grampa's family were discussed often, probably because of the mill, Granny never mentioned her family, and we never saw any of them. They had owned a bakery shop in Burnley, but this was never mentioned. Granny had helped in the shop prior to her marriage, and was a superb baker. She tended to be a little 'nouveau riche' and liked being a mill-owner's wife, so I presume that is why she never mentioned her more humble, but very respectable, upbringing. Dad had a sister Marjorie, who had two daughters, Angela and Margaret. Whilst we were very fond of them, they lived in Staffordshire, so we didn't see them very often.

On Mum's side were Grandma and Grandad Adcroft. Grandma died before Mum married and Grandad died when I was two, so they never featured in our childhood. The family was very close-knit and we often played with our six maternal cousins. Mum was one of seven children. Grandad had longed for a son but all he got was daughters. They had six girls first and then the seventh was a boy, but sadly he died in his twenties. When baby number five was expected, Grandad was convinced that it was a boy. He was making a rag rug, which were popular then and seem to be having a revival at present. He had put one of his four daughter's initials in each corner, leaving the whole of the middle blank ready for the boy. When Aunty Helen was born, he just filled the middle in plain and refused to put Helen's name on it. My Mum was daughter number six, and was always referred to as the 'last disappointment'. Pretty rotten, eh? Mind you, I am not too disappointed that she was born, or else I wouldn't be here either. Grandad was an inspector on the railways, so they tended to move around Lancashire, and had lived in Ramsbottom, Baxenden, and Nelson before settling in Rosegrove, near Burnley.

Cynthia and I had a happy carefree childhood. Mum and Dad were both very even tempered people, who never rowed, or at least we never heard them. They both had easy going personalities, and Dad in particular, was a born comedian. He would make the most outrageous statements, tell jokes, or wind people up and keep a straight face at the same time. Whilst I have inherited the sense of humour, I have not inherited the straight face. If I am winding people up I cannot keep my face straight, and usually spoil the joke! Cynthia was always my ally and most of the time we played happily together. I spent most of my life under her shadow. I was known as Cynthia Clarkson's little sister, rather than my own identity. I thought she was wonderful. Mind you, I tended to get away with murder. All I needed to say was, "well, Cynthia got to do it at this age." Whatever it was, I usually got it, hence she seemed to be my ticket to an easy life. It was also the reason why Cynthia sometimes resented me during our childhood. It came as quite a blow when we were well into adult life to discover this. She said I could wrap Dad round my little finger. She was not wrong. I freely admit it. I was definitely a Daddy's girl. Cynthia tended to be closer to Mum, and also very close to Granny and Grampa Clarkson, as she was the first grandchild.

Our lives were heavily involved with the local Baptist church. Mum ran the Girl's Brigade, Dad was a deacon in the church (a church official), and ran the junior section of the Boy's Brigade. Granny, Mum and Dad were in the choir, and Grampa was the church organist. One of us was at church nearly every evening, and 3 times on Sunday, morning service, afternoon Sunday School (Mum and Dad were teachers), and then evening service when we got older. In retrospect, it sounds oppressive, but it wasn't. The church people were a very supportive extension of our family, and we had lots of good, healthy fun as well. Mum and Dad's special friends were Linda and John; and Herbert and Bertha. They and their children figured greatly in our childhood. In fact, I was named after Mum's friend, Linda. Dad and Herbert were both comedians who wrote and produced pantomimes and sketches that kept everyone amused. Our religious beliefs were an integral part of our childhood, we were brought up to care for others, not to count the cost, and to have a strong sense of moral duty. Religion was never pushed down our throats, and Cynthia and I both came to our own personal belief in later life - myself at nineteen, and Cynthia at thirty.

It can be seen that having a caring concern for others was such a part of our life, that it was no surprise that Cynthia and I ended up as nurses. Cynthia had always wanted to be a nurse, and was so keen that she even had a nurse's outfit at four years old. One year, she wore her nurse's outfit to go to the Sunday School walking day instead of her pretty new dress. (I wore my pretty new dress!) Right from early childhood, she had bandaged her teddies, nursed her dolls and generally bossed us all about in her role as a nurse. If she chose the game, we played hospitals, if I chose, we played schools because I wanted to be a teacher. All the 'patients' were then transformed into pupils as I taught them all. Another favourite game was playing at shops. I used to love being a shoe shopkeeper and Cynthia and I would sell each other shoes. That is probably why I still have a fetish for buying shoes and handbags even now. A photo of my cousins and I was taken when I was two years old, and it shows me with my best patent shoes on, nursing an enormous handbag. Obviously a very early fetish.

Another game that we played was Monopoly, which we played for hours. Cynthia was always the banker, and if the game was drawing close to bankruptcy, she would give a massive cash injection to us both so that we could continue the game. We were often inseparable. When Cynthia got scarlet fever, the doctor wanted to admit her to the isolation hospital, so that I didn't get it, but Mum persuaded him to let her stay at home, on the understanding that we would be kept strictly apart for the incubation period. A bed was put in the front room, with sheets hung over the door to keep the nasty germs inside the room. It was carefully explained to me that I must not go through the sheets or the door into the front room. But I was missing her. Because I was in quarantine, I was not allowed out and subsequently bored. Fortunately, the front room had a large bay window, so I used to climb in through the window to play with her. (Well, I wasn't breaking the rules, Mum had said NOT to go through the door or sheets, and I wasn't doing). We had some close shaves, but I was never caught. I never caught scarlet fever either, so I presume I must be immune.

I hated it when Cynthia first went to school, as I was only two years old and I really missed her. I was quite late at speaking (I know, it's hard to believe now, because since I started talking, I haven't been able to stop!) Apparently, I went round the house looking for her and saying "ere gong? Ere Tiddy gong?" (loosely translated as where has Tiddy gone?) I must explain that 'Tiddy' was my childhood version of Cynthia. I was eternally grateful that I had been born second, as I much prefer my name to hers. At least it is better than Hyacinth, which is what they were going to call her. Cynthia could not pronounce her own name so called herself 'Rufra'- do not ask me why. But my lisping tongue could not say Rufra either, so I called her

Tiddy. We also had a home-help after I was born, and she could not say Cynthia either. She pronounced it Cinifer, and the name stuck. So she rarely got her real name, but got Rufra, Tiddy or Cinifer most of the time.

My nick-names were more obvious - Lindy-Loo, or Lulu. Later I inherited the name Baby Dragon from a television character. Lulu was later extended to Lulu-Pot-Basin, but I cannot remember how it came about, only that it was Cynthia who christened me with it. I suppose she had to get her own back for Tiddy. I used to really enjoy calling her Tiddy in front of her pals. It made her go really wild, when she was trying to be sophisticated and nonchalant. The names her pals gave her were nearly all to do with the shortening of her name to Cyn. So she got Sexy Cyn, Seductive Cyn, Sophisticated Cyn and others that I will leave to your own imagination.

After Cynthia's stories about school, I could not wait to start. The day dawned. I was four years old, and could go to school. I skipped gaily up the steep hill to the school with Mum and Cynthia. I was in the annexe of the school for the first year (which is now the nursery.) It was a low pre-fabricated type of building, and still had a fire range at the front of the class with the most enormous fireguard. I proudly found my desk with a beaming smile on my face. I was grown up at last. No more could Cynthia tease me about being a baby, I was a schoolgirl too. My smile faded when I realised that something was wrong. The rest of the class were crying their eyes out. I really could not understand it. Why on earth were they crying when they were now being allowed to come to school? But cry they did, loudly! Mum watched me closely for signs of distress, but I never shed a tear. I remember thinking that all the other children were big babies, and could not wait for Mum to go. She had prepared me well for school, and I could not wait to get on with my new life, and the business of schooling. All the mothers were putting on brave faces for their offspring, and only one mother started crying when they were asked to leave - mine! She was upset because she thought I did not care about her, and that was why I was not upset. You cannot win, can you? She and Cynthia had obviously done a good job in their preparation.

I loved school, and sailed through my work, always in the top half of the class, and occasionally the top. I had lots of friends, and the school was a very good one, with an excellent pass rate for the eleven-plus examination. I was only in serious trouble once, and it was during an itching powder craze. I had been dared to go and put some itching powder on the teacher's bottom. I am surprised that I agreed, as I was pretty soft. I did the foul deed, but only put it on her chair, the said bottom was rather expansive, and she soon knocked it onto the floor. I was grassed up by John, a boy in my class, along with his pal Derek (will I ever forgive them?) He told the headmaster an exaggerated version of the events. I was punished for it, and made to sit on the front row of the class. This was serious stuff. The class was graded according to ability, and as I had been at the top of the class, I was sat at the back. I was mortified to be put at the front, which in my eyes denoted failure.

I was in the school choir and loved singing, although I had not a strong or particularly good voice. I was narrowly beaten by my friend Jean in the audition to sing the part of Mary in the Nativity Play. Who knows where I could have got to if I had got that part? But then, Jean is not an opera singer so I suppose the answer would be 'nowhere'! But I can dream.

The only other cloud on my junior school days was being an untidy writer and also a left-hander, but I suppose they go together as many left-handers are untidy writers. I was never punished for being left-handed as the generation before me were, but when I finished an exercise, I had to repeat it again with my right hand. Not every teacher insisted on this, but several did, trying to change me into a right hander. My right-handed writing was worse than my left handed writing, so they soon gave up on me. My childhood model teacher was Miss Shaw, who taught me in top infants. I thought she was wonderful.

The end of my junior schooling days came with the eleven-plus results. I knew the date when the results were coming out, but I was petrified that I might have failed. I remember telling Mum that I had tummy ache on the morning of the results, and skiving school. I had to wait for one of my classmates to come home at lunchtime and give me the results. I needn't have worried, as I had passed. I couldn't bear the thought of failing, because Cynthia had passed two years previously, and I have always felt the need to keep up with her. I did not want to surpass her, only to equal her.

This was the stimulus to my working hard in my last year at high school. I was worried that I would not get the same number of 'O' levels as Cynthia. I had got in with a silly crowd in the second year, and wasted most of my secondary education, but I managed to salvage a little by the fifth year. I could not wait to leave school, I did not want to go to sixth form, or on to university or college. It was too much like hard work! So the long standing idea to teach small children went by the board, because I could not be bothered to do further study.

After running through a whole gamut of careers, I applied for nursery nurse training. This had the advantage of being a much less academic course, was offered locally, and involved being with children. It did not go down well with my career's teacher. When I mentioned that I had applied for nursery nurse training, she said, "waste of a high school education, you should go to teacher training college. Next student please." And that was that! Also, the other advantage of nursery nurse training was that a very small wage was offered, unlike other training courses.

I was growing up, but my idyllic childhood was about to come to an abrupt end, and I had to grow up very rapidly. Dad had been ill for most of his life. He had been born with an imperforate anus (no back passage), and had been operated on by the general practitioner, on the kitchen table, in the bathroom. Subsequently, he always had problems with his bowels. He also had a deformed leg and walked with a limp. This gave him constant pain, although he never, ever moaned about it. He used to say that his usual breakfast was a cough, a cup of coffee, three aspirins, and a cigarette or two, to set him up for the day! In his early forties he developed kidney stones and needed surgery. Slowly, he developed kidney failure, and when the stones returned, he could not have further surgery because he had suffered a small heart attack on the previous Christmas Day.

I was in my last week of school, and was having a bit of a lie-in. Mum had gone to work in the old people's home across from our home, and Cynthia had gone to work. She had just completed two years as a cadet nurse and was in the nurse training school for her preliminary block of study. I heard noises in Dad's bedroom and shouted to him. Getting no reply, I went into the bedroom and found him gasping for breath, lying on top of the bed. I was petrified, and froze to the spot. All my first aid training went right out of my head, and I just stood there saying "Dad? Dad? Are you all right?" After what felt like hours, I ran into my bedroom, pulled some clothes on over my nightie, and ran across the road for Mum. Mum came back with me and started artificial respiration and massaging his hands. She said to me "he is not dead, ring the doctor." I remember staring at Mum and thinking what a silly thing that was to say. Of course he wasn't dead, he was my Dad so he could not die, and anyway, he was only forty-five. I rang the doctor but he had left home and had not arrived at the surgery, so Mum told me to ring for the ambulance. But by then, the doctor had arrived.

He rushed upstairs into the bedroom. I waited downstairs and saw the postman coming to the house. He had a letter for me from the nursery training centre to say that I had been given a place on the nursery nursing course. I ran upstairs to tell Mum and Dad the news, but Mum and the doctor were coming downstairs to tell me that Dad was dead. I could not believe it and cried and wailed and said it was not fair. Mum was remarkably calm at this stage. The doctor had warned her three weeks earlier that Dad was 'sitting on a time bomb.' Both the kidney failure and the heart disease could kill him at any time. This had been a great shock to Mum, as Dad had always played down his illnesses. He had constantly laughed and made jokes, so until the doctor told her, she had no idea how ill he was. We were not told about it, so it was a great shock to us when he died. Cynthia was sent for from the hospital. She became suspicious when a nurse tutor came to see her on the ward, to say that Matron wanted to see her immediately. The tutor stayed with her in Matron's office, and then brought her home afterwards.

Cynthia was amazing and just took over everything, she organised the funeral and coped really well for an eighteen year old. Dad had died on the Wednesday prior to the local holidays on the Saturday, so we rushed the arrangements through, and had the funeral on the Friday. Dad was brought to the house in a coffin on the Thursday, but I did not want to go in to see him. Mum agreed with this and did not force the issue. However, at the start of the funeral prayers, my uncle pushed me into the front room, and made me stand next to the coffin, because I was one of the chief mourners. I hated it. That was not my Dad. He would have gone mad about wearing those soppy, satin pyjamas that he had on anyway. I had been to a vampire film recently with Jim, my boyfriend, and anything to do with coffins frightened the life out of me. Ever since Dad's funeral I have had an absolute dread of coffins. I will go and look after the dying, sit with them whilst they are dying, stay with them after they are dead but, the minute they are in a coffin, I run a mile. I always studiously avoid going to the chapel of rest, and say I prefer to remember the person how they were. I am all right once the coffin lid is in place, then I can cope.

Dad's funeral was amazing. The church was packed and the Boys Brigade formed a guard of honour outside the church, whilst the band played the haunting strains of the Last Post. It was very moving. The boy at the head of the parade, although standing perfectly to attention, had tears rolling down his cheeks. Dad had befriended this young man, and he had thought a great deal of Dad. Afterwards, all the Boys Brigades of the Lancashire and Cheshire district had a collection and bought the supplies necessary to build a side chapel in the church in memory of Dad.

It had been a bad year generally for our family, as two of Mum's sisters had died the year before in their forties, and both of their mothers-in-law had died within weeks of their daughters-in-law. Granny Clarkson had died a few years before that but, as I was only young, I was kept away from the funeral and a lot of the upset.

After Dad's death, Cynthia, Mum and I helped each other to come to terms with our loss. Cynthia also had the support of her boyfriend, Edwin, and I had Jim. They were a help to us at this time. Having been such a Daddy's girl, I felt it keenly, so I was glad to have Jim to help me through. I think this early experience of deaths in the family helped me to have a very mature approach to death. I was able to come to terms with death, and work through my own grief and help others through theirs, at a reasonably young age. Having been through the grieving process yourself, you are a lot more empathetic with others.

I decided not to go out to work for the summer months as I had previously planned, so that I could stay at home and help Mum. Well, that was my excuse, it was probably also because I was lazy. The 'O' level results came out, and I felt again the grief of not being able to share precious moments in my life with Dad. At least I had managed to pass enough to get into nursery nursing. Most of the time, Cynthia was working shifts, or out with Edwin, so it was often just Mum and myself around the house. So, my childhood came to an end and I entered the real world - the world of work, which I have not managed to get out of yet, despite trying! Perhaps if this book is a best seller . . . . Oh well, dream on, I didn't make it as an opera singer!!

CHAPTER 2

THE WORLD OF WORK

My first wage was £4 7s 6d (£4.37½p), I gave it all to Mum, and she let me keep it. After that she gave me £1 spending money, £1 for clothes, and 7s 6d for bus-fares. Mum had always believed in encouraging us to budget, so when we started earning we went on clothes' allowance, and had to buy all our own after that - even tights. It was good experience though, and taught us how to manage money.

The nursery nurse course was a two year course leading to the qualification of NNEB, which stood for National Nursery Examining Board. The course started in the January of each year, but there was a curious set-up on our course where you started work in the September. If you were 'suitable', you could progress to the course in January. You were placed in a nursery school without any prior training, and left to it. Depending on how good the nursery was, you got a basic introduction to caring for children. I was fortunate. I went to a very good nursery called Howard Street in Burnley, not too far from where I lived. The head teacher was Miss Corner and she ran a well-organised establishment. I learnt a lot there, and loved watching the children at play. The nursery world is like a microcosm of society, as the children learn to interact with each other, and you see all their personalities developing that will probably continue into later life. The bullies, the managers, the caring people, the down-trodden ones, the happy ones, the sad, the extroverts, the introverts - all can be seen in the playroom.

Watching the children develop and grow was a delight throughout the training. Children have such bright enquiring minds, and are so eager to learn, and explore their surroundings, and find out about life. They often had you in stitches with the comments they made, or things they did. Sometimes it reflected what their life's experiences were. One little boy used to walk round the nursery gently touching things and saying "Johnnie don't touch." We thought it was strange until we found out that John was an unplanned pregnancy. The young parents had bought all their furniture on credit, and Mum had had to go back to work to help keep up the payments. The house was rather a showpiece, and Mum was constantly worried that the furniture would be spoiled by the little boy, hence the ritual in the nursery.

During the first three months 'probation', I had to clean up a child who soiled his pants. I had been absolutely dreading this happening, but I was so concerned for the child who was upset, and wanted to reassure him, that I just got on with it. After that first time it never bothered me again. Had I but known it, it would have set me in good store for being a nurse, but at that stage in my life I was still vowing I would NEVER, EVER be a nurse!

The nursery training centre was situated in an old house on Todmorden Road in Burnley. It was quite large and had obviously been a gentleman's residence in its time. Downstairs, there was a nursery school, that was thought to be something of a showpiece because it was in the grounds of the training centre. It was very pleasant to be able to look out of the windows and watch the children playing during our breaks. Miss Jones was the Principal of the college, and was very much 'the old school.' Lessons were quite formal, and we even had a sort of assembly at the beginning of the college day like a junior school. Coming from my background, I enjoyed the quiet times we had in those sessions, as did a girl who belonged to the Quaker movement, but most of the students thought it was a little old-fashioned. As we got more confident, we were expected to take part in the sessions.

The lectures were loosely divided into education and health. We had a nurse, Miss Denning, for our 'health' lectures, and a teacher, Miss Bowness, for the 'education' lectures. As well as this we had music sessions, drama lessons and cookery lessons. The drama lessons were taken by a larger than life lady called Miss Leslie. She was very theatrical, and made us all go in for an elocution exam, which was quite an achievement with our Lancashire accents. I will never forget her reading "The Naming of Cats" to us. If ever I see or hear the poem now, I am transported back to those drama lessons, and the image of Miss Leslie springs instantly to mind. All the teachers were single ladies, who were dedicated to their profession, although Miss Bowness did marry some years later. The only married teacher we had was Mrs Greenhalgh, the cookery teacher. Oh, what agony, to have to go back to having cookery lessons. I thought I had finished with all that when I left school. We had to trail up to the other end of the town for cookery lessons, as there were no facilities in the training centre. Most people grumbled about this, except me. It was much nearer our house! I am glad that I had got on well with Mrs Greenhalgh, (even though I did not like cooking,) because when I married, we became neighbours.

During our training, we would spend alternate weeks in college and out at the nurseries. We would go to the same nursery for several months and then move. My first nursery was Rosegrove nursery school, which was called 'Burco" nursery by all the locals. This was because it was situated next to Burco's factory, and nearly all the Mums worked there. I stayed here the whole of my first year, and really loved it. The head teacher was tall and willowy, and seemed to float around, but we hardly ever saw her. The guiding light in that nursery was Jean Clegg. She was a small red-headed whirlwind, with a superb sense of humour. I thought she was wonderful, and she certainly taught me a lot.

In those days, all the children had a sleep after lunch, even the four year olds who were ready for school. Or should I say they were put to bed, but they did not do much sleeping. Sleep duty was a nightmare, trying to keep all the lively four year olds quiet, whilst the little two year olds had their sleep, or nap, as we used to call it. The only day that the older ones slept well was when there was potato pie for lunch. Then everyone slept. We used to call it chloroform pie, when cook wasn't listening. When I moved to another nursery, I was not sorry to find that they did not have a sleep period for the older children.

The craze at this nursery was 'Batman' and all the children wanted to dress up in the two Batman capes that we had. There was quite an argument over them at times. All day long, the children were 'flying' around, arms outstretched, cape swinging behind, singing "de de de de de de de de Batman" at the top of their voices. Many of the children had siblings at the nursery, and it was lovely to see their nurturing protective skills coming to the fore. Well, most of the time. Sometimes their bullying, overbearing skills came to the fore too. Sometimes it was reversed. We had a delicate dainty four year old, who eventually became a local beauty queen, and her two year old brother, James. James was a rough, tough, no-nonsense kind of guy who protected his older sister rather than the other way round.

The outdoor playing area was not children-friendly in the late sixties, and was made of ridged concrete, which was quite common. A small fall could result in quite a large cut. One such victim was Darren. Darren was a lively four year old who had an endearing habit of using the word 'love' instead of 'like'. He would say, "I love your shoes Miss Joan," or something similar (Joan often wore gorgeous deep satin pink shoes, left over from a wedding). One day Darren fell and cut his head on the playground floor, and had an inch wide cut on his head. Anyone who has had to stop a scalp wound will know that they bleed like stuck pigs, and Darren's wound was no exception. It was decided he needed a stitch in it.

The nearest Casualty Department was at the far end of Burnley and was a long bus ride, but I was given the job of taking Darren to Casualty. I was not worried about the risk I was taking at the time. Ignorance was bliss. It actually turned out all right, but with my knowledge now, I cringe to think what might have happened to a small boy with a cut head and a head injury. Darren was quite chatty when we set out, but the nearer we got to Hospital, the quieter he got, and cuddled up nearer to me on the bus seat. As we got near, he leaned into me, and said, "I love you, Miss Linda." Oh, it was a lovely feeling. Even though I knew that he meant 'like' really, it made me feel good. He was very brave throughout the time he was in Casualty and cuddled up very closely to me on the way back. In retrospect, I think that we should have been taken to Hospital by car. But no-one thought to offer. I even had to make sure I saved the bus tickets, to claim the money back out of petty cash. What an awesome responsibility I was given. Good job I was a naive sixteen year old! I really enjoyed the nursery work. I was in my element with the children and loved being with them.

Cynthia was well into her student nurse training by now, and had an irritating habit of coming home and describing all the disorders she had been looking after or learning about in school. They all had ridiculously complicated long names, and she would look at me so haughtily whilst she said them. Then, in a totally condescending manner, she would ask "did you enjoy **play** today?" - as if caring for children all day was irrelevant. But one day, I got my own back. Oh revenge is sweet. We had been studying a group of very rare disorders that affect children. They were called inborn errors of metabolism. The commonest one was called phenylketonuria, which often gets shortened to

PKU. In PKU the child has a missing enzyme, which causes problems in the digestive pathways in the body. It also affects the pigment melanin that gives skin, hair and eyes their colour. If it is found out that a child has PKU, a special diet can be given, and the child will have a much better chance in life. If it is not detected, then the child becomes profoundly handicapped, and will always have very blond hair, fair skin and blue eyes. I was fascinated by this group of diseases that could be diagnosed at birth, treated and brain damage prevented.

At night, Cynthia asked her usual question about what had I done at play today. "Oh," I said airily (I would have flicked my hair back nonchalantly as I said it, but I had a short cropped style at the time), "I've been learning about phenylketonuria." Cynthia looked blank, nearly choking on her tea as she asked me what it was. Oh boy, I knew a long name that Cynthia didn't. What joy, what satisfaction! Since then, I have had a life long fascination for inborn errors of metabolism and if people ask me how I became interested in it, I tell them it was because of sibling rivalry!

In the second year, our wage increased to the princely sum of £5 1s 8d (£5.09p). We were sent to a day nursery in Blackburn for six months, as we did not have any day nurseries in Burnley. To reciprocate, Burnley trained the Blackburn nursery nurses. Going to Blackburn involved a long bus journey which I spent knitting. It amused me that at the bus stop there were two shops, one a barbers and one a garden shop. Both were advertising a product called "Growmore" and I often used to wonder if it was the same product both to restore baldness and make your grass grow. I was too soft to investigate.

The day nurseries were run by the social services, rather than the education authorities, and took a much wider age range. In nursery school, the children were from two to five years old, but in day nurseries they ranged from a few weeks old up to five years. The children were divided into rooms by age groups. So there was a baby room, a toddler room and a tweeney room for the oldest age group. (I do not know where they got the name tweeney). With this system, brothers and sisters were separated, which went against the principles of family grouping. Whilst I was in training though, this started to change, and children were looked after in family groups, with a mixture of age groups all in together.

I seemed to spend most of my time in the baby room at Blackburn. The deputy matron ran this room, and she was a stickler for tidiness, especially the pile of terry nappies - this was before the advent of disposable nappies. The nappies all had to be folded with precision, facing the same way. To this day, I still fold my towels ever so neatly, and they are all stacked correctly in the same direction. It doesn't match the rest of the house - that is usually in disorganised chaos. But I cannot get away from this ritual folding. It is probably because, on a bad day, if the nappies were folded wrong, they were knocked to the floor and you had to start again. You didn't often get them wrong a second time! This was the attitude that prevailed in nursing at the time, and I think it rubbed off in some of the nurseries. Often the matron and deputy were trained nurses anyway, and brought some of their habits with them from the hospital.

The babies all stimulated each other in this room, and mealtimes were a nightmare. We had to eat our meals with the children, to make it a more 'normal' environment. Ever tried feeding four babies and yourself all at one go? I now have empathy for those people with quads or quins. It was one spoonful each round the table and then one for yourself. Hopefully, you got to your own turn before baby number one got bored waiting for his next spoonful and threw his dinner on the floor, or even worse, on the next child. During all this, you could guarantee there would be at least one dirty nappy to change. It was certainly not conducive to good digestion, but it probably explains why I eat so fast now. After meals, it was potty time! All the babies were put on the potties and left for a few minutes whilst they performed. At least that was the theory. The reality was more chaotic, as first one, then another, rolled off the potty and scurried away. It was worse if the child had 'performed' as the contents would be all over the floor as well. By the end of potty-time, the babies would all have red rings on their bottoms, where the potty had been. I still have a picture of three of them sitting on their potties. Oh the power I have over these people; the potential for blackmail. It's a pity none of them has become famous (yet)!

One of the older babies learnt to crawl, and had this weird system of crawling backwards. It was very strange to watch and pretty dangerous, as he kept bumping into things behind him, because he could not see. Apparently all the babies in his family crawled like that, so it must have been in his genes. But the strange thing is, as each of the other babies started to crawl, they all crawled backwards. It raises the old argument of nature versus nurture in a new way.

Nursery nursing was a very female dominated profession, with virtually no males setting foot inside the building all day. Often the only male would be the elderly caretaker, which was quite an abnormal situation. As many of the children in the day nurseries were there because they were from single parent families, it was unnatural. It was not until the eighties that men started to appear on nursery nurse training courses locally.

After we had finished at Blackburn, we came back to a local nursery school. Burnley had a lot of nursery schools, built for the working mothers in the local mills, and that is probably why they had no day nurseries. Day nurseries had to be paid for by the parents, whereas nursery schools were provided by the education service. In the sixties, the Burnley nursery schools were more like day nurseries, as the children could attend full time. Also they opened earlier or later than most nursery schools, and were open during the school holidays, although the head teacher got the full school holidays. It was then that I realised that I had made a bad decision in my career. Two of my gang from school, Val and Susan, had both started nursery nursing with me and also realised their mistake. They both went into teacher training soon afterwards and became nursery head teachers for the rest of their careers. But I still could not be bothered to go to College.

The final nursery in my training was Accrington Road, which again was not far from my home. It was another good nursery, and I learnt a lot from the staff there. One of the nursery nurses left whilst I was there to do direct entry Midwifery training. I remember thinking at the time that she was crackers. The most eventful happening that occurred at that nursery was the day the climbing frame fell over. I was on 'playing out duty' that day. The climbing frame was enormous, and just slowly tilted over on its side. Miraculously, no-one was hurt, but there was a lot of 'what ifs' discussed that day. Needless to say, the climbing frame was banned until it could be made more secure.

The end of my training was drawing near, and the dreaded exam loomed. It was two written exams, one in the morning and one in the afternoon. We had about six weeks to wait for the results. The board didn't send you a letter saying whether you had passed or failed, they just sent a pass-list, so you had to wade through to see if your name was there. Thank God I was called Clarkson, and not Young. I skimmed the first page and there I was at the bottom, CLARKSON, LINDA. What a relief. A qualified nursery nurse at last and an added bonus was that Cynthia was still a student. So, for once, I was in front of her. Mind you, she kept telling me I could not put NNEB after my name, as she could put SRN eventually. So what, I thought, I have made it.

My last boss during training, Mrs Heaton, had a vacancy and asked me if I was interested. I felt awful because I liked her and her nursery a lot, but I explained that I wanted to move to somewhere where they didn't know me as a student. She thought that was very sensible, and gave me a good reference for a job at Rockwood Nursery School, near to the nursery training centre.

I thoroughly enjoyed this job. I was working with Jennie with whom I had trained as well so we had some good laughs. During the school holidays, when the head teacher was off, Jennie and I had a brainwave. The books were very expensive and often became soiled so if we painted the pages with clear varnish, we could wipe them over, and they would last a lot longer. I don't know what we did wrong, but a lot of pages stuck together, and we ruined several books. Jennie and I went to an educational booksellers and replaced one book that was totally beyond repair. The head teacher, Mrs Tate, was more cross that we had bought a new book, than she was about the ruined books. We had been dreading telling her, I don't know why because she was a brilliant person to work for.

Another day at the nursery, we lost a child. It lasted for about half an hour, and it was awful, so I cannot imagine what it must be like for parents whose children stay missing. Eventually we found him asleep on the floor behind the settee!

By this time, Cynthia had married Edwin and Mum was doing a spot of 'courting'. After my Aunty Doris died, my Uncle Joe came back to live in Lancashire, to be nearer his dad who had also been widowed. He got a job as Vice-Principal at Bolton Technical College and started taking Mum out for company. Joe had two boys, Rex and Douglas, who were our cousins. Between the four of us, we encouraged the romance, and they married in 1968. So our cousins became our step-brothers. A very complicated family!

Joe had a house at Holcombe Brooke, and, as I was happy working in Burnley, I decided to go it alone. I got a council flat and went to live alone. Mum had nightmares about it, but I was adamant I would be all right. The council let us down though, and I ended up homeless for a few weeks. We had sold the house, Mum had re-married, so I went to live with Grampa Clarkson temporarily. Jennie and I used to have a weekly trip to the council office to badger them into getting a flat. I think Jennie was as delighted as me when I finally got the keys.

The flats were newly built, and the council warned me that nobody else had moved in because there was no gas or electricity available. That did not bother me. I moved in straightaway. Alone in a block of thirty high-rise flats, with no power. I loved it, and never turned a hair. I was just so glad to get into my flat. Mum, Cynthia and Joe had all helped to furnish my flat and it looked very nice. Mum helped me financially, as she felt guilty that she was not supporting me until I got married.

My wage by this time was £39 a month. During a five week month my rent was over £13, so I learnt to budget very carefully. The first Christmas I managed to afford a tiny tree, but couldn't afford any trimmings so Mum made some for me. I kept them for years. I knew I had no opportunity for advancement in the nursery school situation, so I started looking round for a job in a day nursery, where you could rise to the dizzy heights of Matron. I was not particularly ambitious, but I did not like the feeling of never having the chance to improve myself. Besides, I needed the money.

I applied for a job in a day nursery in the next town and got it. There were a good crowd of people working there. Some children came in sadly neglected, and tore at your heart strings. Others were little brats even before they were five. One particular lad, Alan, does not know how lucky he is to have grown up. He was in my room at the day nursery and absolutely drove me nuts. You would just have finished putting all the jigsaws away at home time, when he would tip them all out deliberately on the floor. He could never keep his shoes on, however you tied the laces, and you spent half the day putting his shoes back on. The worst thing of all was his disarming smile when he misbehaved. His younger brother was a much nicer kettle of fish, and was not as difficult to manage. Whilst I have never believed in smacking children, I did come close to murder once or twice with Alan. I just used to walk out of the room when he got to me. In all the years I have worked with children, he was the only one who really got to me.

Also at the nursery was a little girl who was eight months old. She was just about ready to walk, and was still at the same stage ten months later! She just couldn't set off on her own. I looked after her most of the time, but occasionally she was looked after by a colleague called Hilda. I used to try and teach the child to say Linda, but all I got was Hilda. In retrospect, I suppose it was her attempt to say 'Linda', but it certainly rankled at the time. Another child, took his first steps to me, and it saddened me to think that his mother had missed that delightful experience.

The cook at this nursery was a short but large lady, with hardly any teeth. She found out that I lived on my own, and so decided to 'mother' me. I got well and truly fed whilst I was at work. The food was so plenteous that I never made an evening meal in the flat, because I had eaten so much during the day. The meals were free whilst on duty, so that helped my budget too. The usual breakfast would be two weetabix, bacon, egg and the works, plus toast and marmalade. Then there was lunch with a pudding. On a late shift, we didn't get breakfast, but we got afternoon tea instead - jam sandwiches and cake. Whilst this has resulted in a lifelong habit of eating earlier in the day rather than at teatime, it has also resulted in a lifelong battle of the bulge!

After some months at this nursery, I heard about a vacancy as a nursery warden at a day nursery in Colne. This was quite a journey away, but the train station was convenient at both ends of the journey, so I went for it. It was an old chapel, with the babies and a few older ones downstairs, and the older toddlers and the rest of the children upstairs. The deputy matron was in charge of the downstairs and the warden was in charge of the upstairs. I loved the time spent at this nursery. I had two nursery nurses, Jennifer and Moira, and two assistants, Anne and Brenda, working with me and we had two rooms, plus a bathroom.

We all had our own 'family' of four children; I think they gave me all the difficult children. The Dad of one child was a single parent. He was very conscious that he could lose custody if he didn't look after her properly. Every morning, he would give Janet instructions about what she could not do. "No sand Janet, or paint, or clay," he would say, to which Janet would reply, "no, Daddy" very soulfully. I discussed this with him soon after hearing about the morning ritual, but he would not give way. He would not walk through town with her looking dirty. The staff and I had a family council that day. Afterwards, Janet would play quietly until her Dad was well out of sight. Then we changed her clothes from top to bottom, and let her play normally all day. At four o'clock, Janet was bathed, changed and sat reading quietly until Dad re-appeared. Janet was amazing. She never let her guilty secret slip, which for a four year old is pretty good. We did not like deceiving Dad, and we understood his worries. But we also felt that Janet needed to be allowed to play normally.

One year we put on a nativity play for the parents. It is one of the most moving things I have ever been involved in. The children were so clever, and their little voices sang so sweetly.

One of the songs I had taught them, "It Was on a Starry Night", was very difficult to sing, as it had an octave jump in the chorus, but they all managed it. I was so proud of them.

During my time at this nursery, Jim and I got married. There were one or two weddings that year, so we had a theme throughout the upstairs of the nursery and I received presents and cards from the staff and children. I fully expected to be dressed up on my last working day before the wedding but nothing happened. I was usually at the forefront of any larking about when the others got married. Afterwards they said they didn't dress me up because my cousin Geoff was coming to collect me and take me shopping for my wedding present.

One of my favourite ploys was to sneak up on the children when they were unaware of me. This was easy when the children were in the Wendy House. Unfortunately, I overheard something I would have preferred not to one day. Janet and three more children from another 'family' were playing together. Janet was bossing the others about as usual. "I know," said Janet, "let's play at being at nursery. I'll be Mrs Sawley, and you three can be the children." Janet put her hands on her hips and raised her voice, waggled her head and said, "now you children had better behave or else." I was gob-smacked. I had never spoken or behaved like that, so I was quite upset to see myself portrayed like that. I suppose they saw me as the figure of authority in the nursery. Although we were fairly easy going, the other staff always checked with me when making decisions, so I suppose the children had picked up on that. I bet a psychologist would have a field day with it!

After a couple of years, I was finding the travelling difficult. We had bought a house six months after the wedding, still near a train station, but there was still a couple of hours travelling time on top of the working day. I had been to a coffee morning at a nursery school very near home and was told there was a vacancy. I applied, interviewed well and ..... didn't get the job. Somebody 'on supply' got the job - a case of 'feet already under the table'. I was very disappointed as I had talked myself into having a job back in Burnley by then.

I kept looking and found a part-time job in a children's home as a housemother. It was two evenings and two mornings a week, and I worked out that even if I had a family, I could still keep this job. Jim and I hoped to have several children. He was the eldest of eleven, and used to quip that he wanted twelve, to beat his Dad. I used to quip back that after I'd had the first two, who was having the other ten?   We were both very comfortable with children and often borrowed Jim's nephews and nieces to take out. Before I started the job, I was contacted by the other housemother, Joan. She was a foster mother and always had loads of children and it suited her to work evenings rather than mornings. What bliss. I preferred mornings to evenings, so we soon came to an agreement.

On a Sunday morning, the children were all taken to Sunday School, and all the staff hated that job, so when I offered to take them I was well accepted. I could not believe it when they told me the name of the Church. It was my own Church. The only drawback to this job had been working Sundays, and not being able to go to Church. But here I was, working but at Church, and getting paid double time as well! I started the job just before Christmas, but at Easter I went to a service at the headquarters of the European Christian Mission in Rossendale. The speaker was Jean Prior, whom I had heard several times. The talk she gave that night was all about whether you were in the job that God wanted you to do. I sat there feeling smug. Of course I was, I even got paid double time for going to Church. But when I got home, her words kept going through my mind and I could not get any peace. I tried praying about it but just one word came into my mind - midwifery. I was so shocked I looked round the room, thinking somebody else was with me. The word would not go away, and I felt that God was telling me to be a midwife. I had never experienced anything as dramatic as this before, or since for that matter. I let the idea fester over the weekend and then tried it out on people. I told Jim. He thought I was crazy but, after two years of marriage, he had discovered the stubborn side of me, and said to go ahead, because I would do anyway (wise man).

Mum was horrified, "you'll not cope with ordinary nursing, but midwifery is worse. There's blood, and things. You will be hopeless," she said. I tried the idea on a friend who had trained as a nursery nurse with me, but had just been accepted for general nurse training. She laughed hysterically and said, "you, a nurse," and could not say anymore. Cynthia was not impressed either. By this time, I was beginning to think I had made a mistake. The reactions I was getting were not exactly encouraging.

I went to the nearest Maternity Unit that offered Direct Entry Midwifery Training and had an informal interview with the Head of the Midwifery Training School. She did everything in her power to put me off nursing. Shifts, weekends, low pay, studying, etc. etc. But with Cynthia being a nurse, I already knew the down-sides of nursing. Besides, I was already working shifts, and it had not made any difference to our lifestyle. The midwifery teacher told me that all eight places were filled, but I could come on the day that the other eight were coming, and be the ninth applicant. I duly got the interview suit out and trotted along.

There was one other lady waiting. 'A' had two daughters. Prior to her marriage, she had been a student nurse, but when she announced her marriage they were not pleased. Marriage during training was frowned upon, so they said she could get married but put her straight on to night duty for three months. This was fairly standard practice, even if you were not due for night duty. As 'A' was not even going to be allowed a weekend off for the wedding, she gave her notice and left. Now that the children were growing up, she felt that it was time for her to resume her career. In the meantime, she had been a foster mother, and we talked at great length about children. 'A' was one of the eight who had already been accepted on to the course, but the other seven did not come.

We were both accepted, and were sent off for our medical examination. I went in first, and said I would wait for 'A'. However, the nurse sent me off to be measured for my uniform. When I got back, 'A' was still in the Occupational Health department. I was becoming worried as it was quite late. The nurse had told me which cubicle 'A' was in, so I knocked on the window and shouted that I could not wait any longer for her. Unfortunately, at that point, 'A' was being examined by the Doctor. The nurse was horrified and thought I was a peeping tom. She shouted at me to go away, and I realised what I had done. How embarrassing, but at least they could not see who I was. I slunk off home, wishing the ground would swallow me up.

The following Sunday I went to Church, and there was 'A' and her husband at my Church. She explained that they were moving to Burnley prior to her commencing the course, and would be transferring to my Church. Despite the sticky start to our friendship, it augured well for the future, as we would be friends at work and at Church.

Prior to starting the course, I moved to work in an old people's home that was based in the Hospital grounds, but run by the council. The management had changed at the children's home and I was not happy with the way things were going. One day I ended up at the hospital Occupational Health department following a bite by Jim's usually tame ferret. Unfortunately, all the details were written on my nurse's records. Every time I went for check-ups after that, it was mentioned that I had been bitten by a ferret. The staff in Casualty enjoyed the joke too, especially when they saw that the bite was in my groin!

I was a little nervous that I had committed myself to two years training, but was looking forward to this new era in my life. I was twenty-three years old.

CHAPTER THREE

A NURSE AT LAST

September 1st 1972 dawned at last. A bright sunny day, to start a new career. What a silly day to start a new job. The 1st was a Friday, so we worked in School from 8.00 am to 5.00 pm on the Friday, and also Saturday morning until 1.30 pm and then we were allowed to go home until the Monday. We learnt about the course and various rules and regulations and form filling. We also learnt how to make up a hat. Nurses' hats do not come ready folded, but are in a shape similar to the top half of a Maltese cross. You have to fold them into a particular shape and then line up the holes and push a collar stud through. Sounds easy written down, but in reality it is quite tricky, especially as the hat is stiffly starched at the beginning!

Once a crease is made, it stays forever, so if the crease is in the wrong place you have had it. Also, the longer you play with the hat, the less starched it becomes. There is nothing worse than a floppy hat. It spoils your whole day. If you washed your own hat, they never, ever looked right, however much starch you used. Once folded the hats could be very squat or very tall, wide or narrow depending on how you had folded it. Also, the way nurses wore their hats could sometimes tell you a little about them. No two hats ever looked alike, and no two nurses ever wore them in the same way. Some wore them perched forward covering the forehead, others exactly on the crown, others on the back of the head.   The next problem with hats was trying to keep them on.   If you had soft, silky, fine flyaway hair it was hopeless.   You needed an armoury of grips to keep it in place. The morning after the hairwash was agony.   The other problem was being caught in the rain, going between departments.   The hat wilted, usually at right angles and never looked the same again.   The uniform was a lot easier.   Student nurses had moved from the traditional neck-choker dress, with tight collar, to a loose fitting comfortable number, much to our relief.

The Midwifery School was completely separate from the General Nursing School and was housed in a new purpose built Maternity Unit, over the Ante-Natal Clinic. It consisted of three classrooms, a tiny library, offices and toilets.   The desks were arranged in formal rows, but because of the small number in the group, it was quite informal.

I had decided I was not going to tell anyone that I had a sister who was a nurse. I had been Cynthia's little sister for so long, I decided it was now time to be me.   I had heard that our course tutor was to be someone who had attended the same Church as me, so I was worried about acknowledging her and being accused of currying favour.   When we got in the classroom, we had to introduce ourselves.   There were only four of us in the class; 'A', myself and two others, so we were a tight-knit group.

In the first hour, I did not let on that I knew the tutor.   However, at coffee time, she sat with me and proceeded to ask about every member of my family and mentioned Cynthia being a nurse, so my cover was blown. As it happened, I was unable to deny my sisterhood, as total strangers would stop me in the grounds or canteen and ask me what relationship I was to Cynthia. So I remained Cynthia's little sister for the early years of my nursing career. It was quite pleasant in later years when Cynthia had been at home with her children for some years, and people didn't know her. She rang up to complain that she had been introduced as Linda Sawley's sister! At least I could give her empathy - well, after I had stopped laughing, that is.

Although Cynthia had only started in the National Health Service nine years before me, there had been enormous changes in those years. A lot of the hierarchical, rigid discipline and structures were changing. When Cynthia had started in 1963, meals were free and many nurses stocked up on food whilst on duty, to save buying it. If Matron entered the canteen, everyone had to stand and wait for her to be seated. There were rigid divisions in where you sat too. Sisters sat with sisters, staff nurses with staff nurses, students with students, and the doctors had their own separate dining room with waitress service.

On the ward a student spent virtually the first three months of their training in the sluice washing bedpans and testing urine. Then they were promoted to assisting with bed-baths, and the "obs". Obs was short for observations, and meant taking the patient's temperature, pulse, respirations and blood pressure. Carrying out wound dressings and giving out medicines was saved for much later in the training. Yet when a student went on night duty, they were in charge of running the ward, and had to do everything, with only a visiting Sister supervising. On the day shift, at the beginning of the shift, jobs were given out depending on seniority, and were purely task allocation. You did all the "obs" or all the bed-baths. With this system, a patient could see eight or ten nurses per shift. One to attend to bedpans, one for bed-bath, one for "obs", one for dressings, one to bring meals, and so on. There was no continuity of care at all. By 1972, a lot of these rituals were breaking down, and certainly we all ate in the same canteen, albeit the doctors were screened off from the mere nursing staff and still got waitress service. By 1972 we had had to start paying for our meals, too.

On the first Monday of the course, we went across the hospital grounds to another School of Nursing and joined up with the 'R' group of students. (Each intake of students had a letter.) We were to do an introductory block of eight weeks, introducing us to the rudiments of nursing. Uniform had to be worn in school and the four student midwives stuck out like a sore thumb. Everybody else had a green belt, to show they were a first year student nurse (green being a very suitable colour)! Whereas we had white belts because we were first year student midwives. Straightaway we were noticed, and lumped together with comments like, "oh yes, those are the midwives." The introductory block was previously called the PTS or preliminary training school and most of the ward staff and tutors still called it PTS. We were taught in a brand new purpose built school at the bottom of the hospital grounds. Because we were a large group, (twenty-eight in all), we had to be taught in the lecture theatre. This was a very large room, with theatre-type plastic seats and had no external windows or doors. Thus it was very stuffy, depressing and uncomfortable. There were quite a few married women in the group, so we tended to stick together. One of the general students had an older sister who was a nurse whom everyone knew, so she was her 'little sister'. We had great empathy for each other!

The general school was a lot bigger than the midwifery school. It had five classrooms besides the lecture theatre. One of them was set up as a practical room, so that skills could be learnt in the safety of the classroom, without harming patients. There was also a library and the usual offices. The beauty of the general school was that classes ran from 9.00 am to 4.15 pm, not 8.00 am to 5.00 pm like the midwifery school, so it was a little easier. The Principal Tutor was quite a character. He had a fascination for words and their meanings. He would always encourage you to break down a medical word to understand its meaning, for example anaemia would be separated into <u>an</u> and <u>aemia</u>. <u>An</u> means without, and <u>aemia</u> means blood, so anaemia means literally, "without blood". He used to get carried away sometimes and ask "What is an electrolyte?, Why is it called an electrolyte? Why not a carolyte or an electrobroom?" We used to laugh at him behind his back. Yet nowadays if I want to understand the meaning of a medical word, I start breaking it down into small components. So, although I laughed, I learnt the lesson.

Because of the large numbers in the group, classroom teaching was quite formal, and the tutors were called by their surname.

We had a group tutor who had two very lively small daughters. She kept us amused telling us about their antics. As well as tutors, there were people called clinical teachers. They were experienced nurses, who had moved into the Education Centre (previously called the School of Nursing). They mainly worked on the wards, working with student nurses and doing ward-based teaching. They also worked in the practical room, and did some classroom teaching. They spent more time with the pupil nurses who were doing a two year training to become Enrolled Nurses. We student midwives had joined up with nurses who were doing a three year training to be State Registered Nurses.

Two of the clinical teachers taught us more than the others. The most memorable session they did was on death and dying which they did together. Unfortunately, they kept crying during the session, and as soon as one settled down, the other one would start crying! But that was exceptional. They were both lovely ladies who we admired a lot. Another character was the tutor who had brought Cynthia home when Dad died. He had a terrific sense of humour, and his own inimitable way of explaining things.

During the eight weeks we were introduced to nursing, as both a science and an art. We learnt about anatomy and physiology - how the body is made up and how it functions. Much of the teaching was in lectures, but we also did practical work. Bed-making was one practical session. It looks so simple when you know how, but oh the difficulties when you are learning. Sheets look lop-sided, blankets look bulky, pillows do not look comfortable. The hospital corners are a nightmare in themselves, where the sheets and counterpanes have to be folded in a particular manner, to hang neat and tidy. It would not do for Sister to see untidy hospital corners. She would be likely to uncover the whole of the bottom of the bed, to show her disapproval, and to make sure that you had to re-make the bed.

A ritual that was also involved in bed-making was placing the draw-sheet in the bed. The draw-sheet was a throw back to Victorian days when linen was in short supply. A small narrow sheet, about the size of a baby's cot sheet but longer, was placed in the bed, usually with a blue plastic sheet under it. The cotton draw-sheets were originally quite long. When the patient soiled it, either from body fluid, food or wounds, the sheet could be drawn through towards the other side, until the patient was on a clean patch of sheet. The soiled part would then be tucked under the mattress, hence the name draw-sheet.

You can imagine what state those sheets must have been in, but they did save linen. By the time I was using them, they were merely used to prevent having to change both of the large bed sheets if there had been an accident, but their old name lived on. Also, by 1972, the undersheets were mainly made of thin blue plastic, whereas previously they had been made of thick orange rubber. The orange rubber undersheets used to be quite awkward and heavy and often started to disintegrate. They had a peculiar smell when you washed them and they were often festooned all round the bathroom to dry. The thin blue plastic under-sheets were heralded with delight, but there was a new unthought of hazard with these. Because they were plastic, they often produced static electricity. Some people were not affected by static, but I was. Bed making was often a nightmare, especially on the modern beds, as I was constantly getting shocks, some of them quite deep and very painful. It was not just the bed making either. I often got shocks if I touched other people, or the panel on the lift shaft.

Another task to be learnt was the bed-bath. To show how embarrassing this could be, one of the group had to be put through the agonies of the bed bath, suitably clad in modest swimwear. Fortunately, there were no men in our class, so it was not too embarrassing. First the tutors showed how it could be done to cause minimal embarrassment, and then it was our turn. It was very difficult to perform this task with dignity, and without dissolving into giggles or hysterics in class. In real life, it was far easier, because you were striving to make your patient more comfortable and less embarrassed. Each part of the body had to be washed, rinsed and carefully dried, without leaving the patient exposed or shivering.

Mouth care was another skill to be learnt. This entailed cleansing the mouth with swabs that had been dipped into a pink fizzy solution. Making us carry out the task on each other made us realise how the patients felt. A lot of gagging noises were heard. It was even funnier when we had to clean each other's teeth with toothbrush and toothpaste.

One of the most nerve racking experiences is giving an injection. We learnt the theory in school and then practised injecting water into oranges. It is definitely not like the real thing! Giving the actual injection looms before you as a major incident, but the actual skill of preparing an injection is very difficult too, requiring great manual dexterity. First of all, you have to check you have got the right drug. No mean feat, as the writing is very small. Some drugs come in powder form, so you have to draw up sterile water into a syringe and squirt it into the powder and make sure that it is mixed thoroughly. Other drugs come ready mixed in a glass ampoule. The top of the ampoule has to be snapped off before it can be used. A metal file is given to assist in sawing the top of the ampoule off, but the file is often lost, and also it takes time. Most nurses snap the ampoules with their fingers, and also carry the scars where the ampoule has cut their finger. It was forbidden to do this, but you did it anyway. Alternatively, the ampoule was covered with the hem of your dress or apron, to snap it without injuring yourself. Whenever you prepared the injection, it all had to be done without the introduction of any infection.

There were also many different types of injections. Some of them were placed into the tissues just under the skin, at an angle of forty-five degrees. Other injections were given straight into the muscle, at a ninety degrees angle. Some injections were given very deeply and in a Z formation, such as iron injections. The site for the injection had also to be chosen with care. If the wrong place is used on the thigh or buttock, it can damage the sciatic nerve, which can cause paralysis and leg wasting.

We also had to learn how to test urine. For this skill, we all had to provide our own sample to practise on. The urine is tested by dipping a thin plastic stick covered with reagents into the urine, and waiting the prescribed time before reading the result. The tutors got quite excited if any of us had anything abnormal showing in our urine!

Towards the end of the introductory block, we were allowed out on to the wards for half a day at first, then a full day, then a night shift. It gave us time to get used to trying our skills out on real patients with the support of tutors and clinical teachers. I was a laughing stock on my first ward, as I put the bedpan in back to front. At the end of the eight weeks we were let loose on the wards. As we were training to be midwives, we went back to the Maternity Unit, rather than on to the general wards as our colleagues from the introductory course did.

Back we went to our little midwifery class, and the comfort of only having four in a class. Sadly, it was also back to school lessons from 8.00 am to 5.00 pm again. After a short block teaching us the basics of midwifery, medical terminology and nursing care, we went on to the wards. Each week we had a study day, and as we started at 8.00 am each week with a test, it was a great encouragement to study the lessons we had learnt the week before. This weekly study day format became old-fashioned and not highly thought of in the educational world. The general school had gone onto systems of blocks every three to six months, with no visits to school in-between. I preferred the weekly visits to school. Because of the test, you remembered the theory far more, and also if there was anything worrying you, you could discuss it with the tutor in the classroom. When it was three to six months between blocks of study, most of the theory was forgotten, and sometimes you sank or swam on the wards.

The senior midwife tutor was the lady who had interviewed me. She was a small, elegant, gentle spoken lady, who inspired you by her devotion to midwifery. A single lady, she shared a house with another senior midwife on the labour ward, or delivery suite as it had been renamed. Where one was small and dainty, the other was large, lively and brusque. If she approved of you, she would whack you on the backside in passing. I suppose nowadays that might be frowned upon, but we took it as a big sign of favour in those days, and nobody took offence.

During the first three months on the Maternity Unit we rotated through the various departments. We visited postnatal wards, the delivery suite and the ante-natal clinic, so that we could get an all round picture of midwifery care. The staff on the wards consisted of midwifery sisters, staff midwives, enrolled nurses, auxiliaries and other students. As we were direct entry midwives, we were learning basic general nursing skills as well as trying to learn midwifery skills. A difficult task. Some of the midwives did not like direct entry midwives, feeling that all midwives should be registered general nurses as well, so sometimes we were treated with impatience or indifference. But these attitudes were few and far between. I worked with one midwife quite a lot. She was a direct entry midwife too, so understood exactly how I felt. All the midwives rotated on to different wards and departments too, and I often seemed to rotate with her at the same time. She became my 'special midwife' for the whole of my midwifery career and always seemed to be around when I needed her

She arranged my first injection. I had been absolutely dreading it and had confided in her. The longer it was since the theory lecture, the more I was worried about it. Eventually, we had a patient in who had diabetes mellitus and needed insulin injections. Whilst she was in hospital, she preferred the nurses to give the injections in different sites than usual, that she could not reach herself.

The lady offered to let me practise on her, but I stood for what seemed like hours, poised with the needle in my hand, not daring to push it into her arm. Eventually she urged me to hurry up, because her meal was going cold! That did it, I positioned the needle carefully and pushed it into her skin. She did not scream, cry or faint, so I eagerly asked if I had done all right. "I've had better," she said, "but you were all right". I felt terrific. I had done it at last, and could not wait to tell my friends and family, who were largely unimpressed. Only a fellow nurse can appreciate the feelings at this time.

Once I had done the insulin injection, I felt confident to try an intra-muscular injection, which goes into the muscle instead of just under the skin. We had another lady who had an infection and was being nursed in the isolation cubicle. She needed an anti-biotic injection, so I was sent to give it. I went bravely to give the injection. With greater confidence than I felt, I gave the injection, and then asked if it had been all right. "It was fine" said the patient. "Oh good," said I, "it was my first." "Well," she said, "you did very well."

I reported back to the midwife on my prowess, and she looked at me curiously. "You didn't tell her it was your first injection, did you?" she asked. "Yes, I did, why?" I replied. "Because she needs another one as well," she said. Oh dear. That poor brave lady did not even flinch when I turned up again, knowing that it was only my second injection. A martyr to the cause of the nursing profession.

The method of recording nursing care was very basic in those days in many hospitals. In our unit, a ward book was kept and most of the information was written in it. A general summary was made in the report book. The newly delivered mothers or poorly mothers and babies got a mention but those who were progressing normally only got a collective mention. "All remaining mothers and babies are satisfactory" was a common report. During my training, individual cards were introduced throughout the country called Cardex. After this, each mother had her own card file that was much more individual and satisfactory. The midwives did not think so. They just thought that it was a lot more paper work, especially if there had been several admissions during a shift. Instead of having to write a one-line report about each new mother and baby, they had all the forms to fill in. Despite the extra paper work, it made nursing care a lot more reliable. You knew exactly what had happened to a patient by reading through the Cardex, even when you had been on your days off.

The three months of normal midwifery went quickly. We were encouraged to 'witness' as many births as we could during this time. We had to witness thirty births before we were allowed to start delivering them ourselves, with assistance. When a mother was progressing to the second stage of labour, or starting to push, she would be asked if she minded students witnessing the birth. The mother by this time could not care less who saw the birth, and would have said 'yes' to anyone, as long as she could get on with pushing out her baby. If the mother said 'yes' the midwives would ring round the wards asking if anyone needed a 'witness' birth. You ran down to delivery, donned a gown and mask and ran in to the delivery room, to watch the birth. It doesn't happen now, as detailed birth plans are made between the mother and the midwife. But there is only one way a student midwife can gain experience. That is by first watching and then helping.

The first birth I watched was magical. We were on a study day, when the Delivery Suite rang. We all ran into the delivery suite and a midwife told us which room to go to. We made a bee-line for that room donning gowns and masks. We were just in time. We positioned ourselves at the bottom of the bed. The midwife showed us the bulge of the baby's head, stretching the skin between the lady's vagina and her anus (back passage). The bulge went back between contractions. With each contraction, the head moved further until the tip of the head could be seen at the entrance to the vagina. The midwife applied pressure to the head to prevent the mother being torn, and the head was then allowed to be born between contractions. As the head was fully freed, the baby's head did a ninety degree turn, a phenomena that never failed to amaze me. With the next contraction, the baby's body usually slithered out.

What a heart-stopping miracle, to see this child start to breathe, after nine months living inside the mother, made from the fusion of the largest and the smallest cell in the human body. What a joy to watch those first precious moments as a newly delivered mother sees her new-born baby. "Is it all right?" and "what sex is it?" were always the first two questions the mother asked in those days. With modern ultra sound scans nowadays, parents often know the sex of the baby, so some of the mystique has gone. But also, some of the birth defects are detected on scans and parents are forewarned so that the shock of a deformed baby is not as common.

Throughout the birth I had been absolutely riveted by what was going on. I was also fascinated by the third stage of labour where the afterbirth or placenta was delivered. By now, under the hot lights in the delivery suite, and with a gown and mask on top of my uniform, I realised that I was feeling very light headed and sickly. I got myself out of the room as quickly as I could. Midwives smiled knowingly as I came into the staff room, as if I could not cope with the birth, but it was the heat that I could not stand. I have never been very good in hot weather and often feel faint. The Delivery Suite was always far too hot and I always found it a difficult environment to work in.

We slowly returned to the classroom, overawed by our experience, and discussed the process that we had witnessed. As the other three had had children of their own, I was the only one to whom it was a totally new experience. I was on cloud nine for days, constantly reliving the experience in my mind.

At the end of the three months, we returned to the general side, and met up with our cronies from the introductory block. Our experiences were very different, as they had all been on surgical wards, but a lot of discussions and comparisons went on anyway. We undertook a 'medical' block of study, where we learnt about conditions such as heart disease, lung disease and bowel disease. The lectures were to prepare us for going out on the wards, and some of the conditions that we might meet.

After the block of study, we were let loose on the patients again. As I was a student midwife, I only worked on women's wards, much to my relief. We did one month on a medical ward, one month on a surgical ward, one month on a children's ward, to give us a taste of general nursing.

My first ward was a large female medical ward, containing patients who had problems like heart and chest conditions, high blood pressure, anaemia, strokes and anything else that did not require an operation. It was also the ward where my sister had been a ward sister until recently, so I was recognised by all and sundry. The wards were long and narrow, with beds on either side - so called Nightingale Wards. It's pretty daunting to have to walk all the way down the ward for the first time, especially when you are wearing uniform for the first time in public. It also caused problems because we had different uniforms. It amused the ladies that they were being looked after by student midwives, and many jokes were made.

It was even more fun on the surgical ward. Because I had been on the Maternity Unit, I had become quite an expert at shaving ladies 'down below'. In the seventies all ladies in labour were given a pubic shave for cleanliness reasons. It caused embarrassment at the time, discomfort a few days later, and further embarrassment later, as regrowing hair is very itchy and it is not a place you can scratch in public! When the Sister found out I was a student midwife, I had to do all the shaves that were carried out before operations. The surgical ward I was on had a lot of different specialities, there was general surgery, gynaecology (women's problems), renal (kidney), vascular (blood vessels) and dental operations. The ward was very busy with a rapid turnover each day. There were ten to twenty waiting list admissions each day, besides the emergency admissions. All the patients had to be interviewed and examined by the doctor, and details taken for the nursing records. Then they had to have the appropriate part shaved before going to theatre.

When it was a gynaecological (gynae) list, it was chaos. I was always given the gynae patients by the senior Sister, who was a stern, serious disciplinarian. One day, I was given 'shaves' as usual. I started in the side ward, who were all gynae patients and when I had finished them I moved to the main ward. The first lady was having an operation under her arm, so I shaved the armpit. The next lady was having a stomach operation, so I shaved her from 'nipple to knee'. At the next bed, I went behind the screens, and the patient laughed when I came in. She was sitting on top of the bed, but pulled her nightie up, took her knickers off, lay on her back, put her heels together and opened her knees. "I know what you've come for, I've been in this ward before," she laughed. Relieved that I hadn't to explain things yet again, I started to shave her 'down below'. Halfway through the shave, I asked her what operation she was having, "I'm having my wisdom teeth removed", she said. I froze mid-stroke. It is to my credit that I did not cut her in ribbons. "Why are you letting me shave you down here then?" I asked. "Oh, it's the routine on this ward, you always get shaved whatever you come in for." At that point, Sister came in and stared at us. "Have you a minute Nurse," she said, with her sternest look. My heart sank. I followed her out of the screens and down to the office. "Do you know what operation that lady is having?" she said sternly. "Yes, I do now, but I didn't when I started," I replied lamely. She gave me a lecture about not checking my patients, and making a patient suffer unnecessarily, then she sent me back to finish the shave. Suitably chastened, I slunk off down the ward back to the patient, but I could have sworn I heard a hearty laugh coming from Sister's office. I never lived it down with the patients. They teased me mercilessly. The patient herself had a cartoon brought in by a relative. It showed an artist painting pubic hair on to a nude statue. The patient kept it pinned up on the back of the bed, for all to see. I was glad when that group of patients went home. It taught me a good lesson, though.

The other ward I worked on during this period was the Children's surgical ward. It was not a 'Nightingale' ward, but consisted of lots of small bays and cubicles. It also had a room that was used as playroom, dayroom, school room and dining room. The sister was a lovely, gentle silver-haired lady, whom the children loved. Her lovely lilting voice could be heard calming the patients who were frightened, although she could also be stern if necessary.

Following the time on the 'general' side, we went back to the Maternity Unit. This time we started to learn about what complications can occur in midwifery. Study days were still weekly from 8.00 am to 5.00 pm with the proverbial test at 8.00 am We visited each ward on rotation, learning the basic skills of midwifery, doing the 'obs' and caring for the mothers and babies. One Mum had had a caesarean section and was very uncomfortable. On the third day, her breasts had filled with milk and they were very engorged and sore. Added to this, the baby could not latch on to her breast for feeding, because she was so engorged and she desperately wanted to breast feed. On the third day after childbirth, a woman's hormone levels are at an all-time low, and she often gets very weepy and emotional. It's often called the "third day blues" by midwives. This poor lady sat on the bed in tears on her third day. I felt helpless to know what to do. In the end I sat down by her on the bed, and put my arm around her and talked to her. I also ended up crying with her! She cheered up, though, and was soon able to cope with feeding her baby.

Before we knew it, the first year of our training was complete. Sadly, towards the end of the first year, two of the students left so our little group was halved. Another group of enrolled nurses had started a course six months after us, but they tended to have lectures on their own, though they were taking their exams at the same time as us.

At the beginning of the second year we were joined by two nurses who were qualified SRN's. They only needed to undertake one year of training, because of their general nursing experience. Again, we were a small knit group, who became great friends. Nurses have to develop a relationship with patients and colleagues very quickly. Patient turnover has become increasingly rapid. Patients in hospital are at their most vulnerable, if they have had an illness that has brought them suddenly into hospital for treatment. Alternatively, if they are having an operation, it often makes them review their life and think serious thoughts. Patients will often ask the most searching and difficult questions. They usually have an uncanny instinct of asking the most junior and most inexperienced person on the ward, who is usually out of their depth. Questions like, "am I going to die, nurse?" and "have I got cancer?" are difficult at the best of times, but more so when it is the first time you are asked. Often in the small hours of the night patients who cannot sleep will confide their innermost secrets and fears to the nurse, who can be a total stranger. Mind you, sometimes it's easier to confide in a stranger, than talk to relatives and friends.

During training, a placement on a ward could be between two and eight weeks. Thus you tended to be able to fit into any team, and work alongside people very quickly. Friendships could be very close for a short time, then you moved on, and never saw the person again.   It   tended   to   encourage   superficial relationships, but not always. Life-long friendships have been made amongst nurses especially those in the same training group.

In the second year of our training, we started all over again, because of the SRN's who had joined us, by studying basic midwifery.   Here, 'A' and I had the advantage over the other two. We were reinforcing learning and it came easier to us the second time. The structure of the second year of the course was three months introduction, then three months working out in the Community, then six months back in hospital studying abnormal midwifery.   For the community part of our course, we had to have a 'phone at home, and be a car owner/driver, or we had to live in at the nurse's home, for easy contact. I duly applied to have a phone installed, and started taking driving lessons. I hated every minute of them. I had had a teacher recommended to me, whose wife worked in the hospital. He had formerly taught bus drivers. If ever I was not sure about whether I could get through a gap with the car, he would pipe up, "you could get a double decker bus through there." That became a standard phrase, and one I found I kept using when Jim learnt to drive years later. The lessons stumbled along, I could only afford one a week. By the following week I had forgotten what he had taught me the week before. In exasperation, he used to let me go round corners in fourth gear so that it would stall, because I steadfastly forgot (or was too lazy) to change gears. It taught me a lesson at long last. His other bribe was to let me drive on the by-pass for a while if I had not made any mistakes. This was driving! Foot down, no gears for ages, and the feeling of really moving.

The big day came at last. Nervous as anything, I took my test and failed. Oh, well, I consoled myself, everyone fails first time. I was wrong. A boy at Church who started learning at the same time as me passed a month later, first time. He was only seventeen years old, and his Dad forced him to drive to work in the rush hour, both morning and night. I, however, carried on with the lessons, whilst Clarence got more and more exasperated. One day, I was telling him a little about my job and he screwed his face up and said he could never do my job. I replied that I could never do his job, but then on reflection, I said, "still, I suppose each new pupil is a challenge to you." "Yes," he quipped back "and this is my finest hour." Humph, men!

I failed the second test, too. On the day of the third test, everything was perfect, fine weather, half day closing, children all at school. All was well with the world. I drove really well, so was pretty hopeful. I failed again, on every bit of basic driving. It was at the end of the month, and I am sure they had passed their quota for that month. I was very disgruntled and decided to give up. I did not need to learn any more, as I had already been on Community. But then I worked out how much I had spent and decided to have one last test. The day was disastrous. It was pouring with rain. It was the day before the local holidays, so all the mills had closed early, schools had closed, people were rushing about everywhere and to cap it all, Clarence had bought a new car. I had only had one lesson in it.

The driving examiner was a new one. It was his first day on his own. I think he was just as nervous as I was. I read the number plate easily and got in the car. "Do you suffer from any nervous disabilities?" he asked. "No" I replied, "only when taking driving tests." He politely smiled and told me to proceed. I put the car into gear before I realised that I had not switched on the engine! "Do you see what I mean?" I asked. He reassured me that the test had not started yet, and told me to relax. I then proceeded to kangaroo hop the car all the way to the first junction. Well, that's it, I thought blown it again. Might as well sit back and enjoy my very last drive. We got back to the test centre, and he asked me some very badly worded highway code questions. Oh well, I rationalised, I have never failed on the highway code before. Then came the result - I had passed. I started crying and told him how important it was as I was a midwife. He seemed pleased, too. But what a wally I must have seemed. I can still blush at the embarrassment of it.

However, passing the driving test came after the time spent on community. A more important event happened prior to community - that which all nurses fear and dread. I went on 'the wrong side of the blanket', and became a patient myself. During childhood I had managed to avoid hospitals except at two for the X-ray and at six for a wasp sting in my mouth. During a routine dental X-ray, my dentist had found that I had two fully grown supernumerary (extra) teeth, above my front teeth. He got quite excited about them and brought his colleagues in for a look. "Oh good," I commented, "my Dad had a third set, and they grew down when he lost his second teeth." All the dentists laughed, and I realised I had said the wrong thing. "If yours start erupting, they'll come out through your nose, they're upside down." Trust me, born awkward again, couldn't even get my third set of teeth right. The decision was made to let them be but, during my first year of training, I had noticed one of my front teeth was crooked. They decided to operate and remove them, taking out all four wisdom teeth that were impacted, too. I wanted to have the operation done during my holidays, so that I did not have any sickness during my training, but I was persuaded to take time off.

I was admitted on the Sunday, for surgery Monday and went on the surgical ward. The Sister was superb with me and laughingly said I would reduce the average age. The average age of the patients was eighty-two that day. It was more like a Care of the Elderly ward. The Nursing Officer for the surgical unit came to visit me. He was a lively chap, who always had a cheery word or a funny comment. He talked about having surgery and asked if I was frightened. There was only one thing worrying me. When Cynthia had had surgery whilst a student nurse, she had been quite violent coming round from the anaesthetic, thrashing around with her arms, and using language that she never ever used when awake. As she was a patient on the same ward where she had been working the day before, it was doubly embarrassing. That was my only fear, but it was unfounded. I was popped on the trolley and taken to theatre. That journey lying on the trolley, looking at the ceiling is very strange, and feels very long. Added to this, if you have had a pre-medication injection, you are likely to be dry-mouthed and feeling a little woozy. I had also had an antibiotic injection of a thick white substance that hurt! Once in the anaesthetic room, the dental surgeon came out to talk to me. The anaesthetist was also asking me questions and it is so hard to answer when your mouth is dry. Shortly afterwards, I drifted off to sleep, and woke up back on the ward.

I remember an awful taste in my mouth - it remained for weeks afterwards. I moved my tongue gingerly round my mouth, and felt lots of stitches dangling everywhere, and a swelling on the roof of my mouth. I felt further back, but there did not appear to be any damage where the wisdom teeth were. I drifted in and out of sleep, punctuated by retching and vomiting blood. I also had pain in my calves. In my semi-conscious state, I became worried about both facts. Blood stained vomit and pain in calves were serious. It did not register that I had been on a theatre table for hours. That is probably why my calves ached, or that I had swallowed a lot of blood after a dental operation, and that is why I was vomiting blood. No, nothing so simple when you are a nurse. You know too much, and think the worst.

I did not look in the mirror the first day. On the second day, I bravely looked in the mirror and this awful face looked back at me. I looked like Plug in the Beano comic, after a fight. I had black eyes, swollen and bruised jaw, nose pushed up, and fat lips. I also had a clot on the roof of my mouth, so I tended to keep my mouth open, with my tongue hanging out. I looked and felt dreadful. When the dentist came to see me, I complained that my calves hurt more than my mouth! He explained that I would have to come back in again for my wisdom teeth, as it had been so difficult to remove my supernumerary teeth, that he'd given up. One tooth had had to be removed from my nose, so the original dentist had been right.

I was allowed home on the Wednesday morning, and the next day I went to visit my General Practitioner. He was a real gentleman who unfortunately died very young following a heart attack. The doctor didn't know I was going into hospital, so when I walked into the surgery, he jumped up and said, "oh, my dear, who has done this to you?" When I replied "the dentist" he laughed and sat down. I suggested that he go and announce it in the waiting room, because I had been studiously avoided, and given very dirty looks by all the other patients. They obviously thought I had been in a fight!

On the Sunday, 'A' rang me to ask why I had not been to Church that morning - it had been a special service. I reminded her that I had just come out of hospital. She told me that a man was coming to speak that night, who they were thinking of inviting to come as the new minister, and there would be a congregation vote following the service. I decided to make the effort and go, wrapping a thick scarf round my face, both to cover it up and keep it warm. The prospective preacher got up into the pulpit. He wore half moon gold rimmed glasses, at the end of his nose, and looked over the top of them at the congregation. "You're a miserable looking lot, it won't hurt any of you to smile," he said. I felt like jumping up and telling him that it would hurt me and that it was impossible for me to smile. I decided that I disliked him on sight. When it came to the vote, I abstained! Little did I know that I would become very involved with his family and am Godmother to his youngest child. It's a good job we don't always go by first impressions!

Another very important incident also happened before I passed my driving test - one of the most precious moments of my nursing career. I delivered my first baby. I was doing a stint of night duty in the summer and had already witnessed more than thirty births. I was promised that when a 'suitable' case came up, I could deliver it. By 'suitable', the lady had to have had a perfectly normal pregnancy, preferably with a history of a previous normal delivery, and a normal labour so far. The notes were also scrutinised for any previous medical or family history of ill-health or abnormal births. By this time, you can see that the numbers of births that qualified were few and far between. At the time when I trained, midwives also warned you about caring for redheads. People with red hair were supposed to be notorious for being 'bad bleeders' and a haemorrhage could occur during labour. In modern research based practice, this has probably been discounted, but it was a warning that was passed down from midwife to midwife through the years.

Eventually a suitable patient was chosen. I was assigned a senior midwife and I was glad that she would be supporting me during this nerve-wracking experience. It was the lady's first baby and her labour progressed normally. I built up a relationship with her during the hours prior to the birth. Eventually she said she wanted to push. We checked her over, and confirmed that she was in the second stage of labour. We got the equipment ready, then positioned her comfortably in the bed, with her legs in the air, and feet resting on our hips. Between pains, we explained how to make the most of her contractions, by pushing down into her bottom, and not making a noise into her throat. It is the easiest thing in the world to groan into your throat whilst pushing, but the energy all goes into your throat, instead of to the body, and prolongs labour.

Eventually the baby's head started to crown. I put my fingers on top of the head to control the birth of the head. The midwife held on to the baby's head with me. I was surprised at the force needed to hold the head back, so that it can be delivered slowly. The head was born carefully, then the body slithered out. A beautiful, healthy, male specimen. We sucked his air passages out and wrapped him in a soft towel before giving him to Mum for a cuddle. Next, we returned to Mum to deliver the placenta (afterbirth).

Once I had delivered the baby and placenta, we checked Mum to see if there was any excess bleeding, then looked at the baby. A very detailed head to toe examination is carried out to check for any abnormalities, and then the baby is weighed, given namebands, bathed and dressed. Babies can lose heat very quickly at birth, so very great care is taken. Often the Mum would breast feed at this stage. Nowadays this is done the minute the baby is born. Once the baby was clean and warm, the Mum and baby went up to the ward. I was ecstatic. I could not believe I had actually delivered a baby. Well, the midwife and me anyway. The midwife laughed as I relived every second, but brought me down to earth with a bump by reminding me about all the paperwork. What a thrill to put my name in the section marked 'Delivered by'. Once I had filled all the paperwork in, the midwife countersigned it all, and filled in the birth registers and other forms that I was not allowed to do because of my student status. Then I was free to pop up to the ward to check on my mother and baby. They were both fast asleep. It was my Aunty Marjorie's birthday.

All was well with the world. I went home from night-duty in a whirl, then remembered that I had booked a two hour driving lesson before I could go to bed. I waited for Clarence on the main road, barely able to contain myself. I saw the Minister from church driving towards me and waved madly at him. "Hi, guess what?" I gasped, "I've delivered a baby." "Oh very nice," replied the embarrassed Minister, as he drove on. By then Clarence was arriving. I told him my news and he suggested cancelling the lesson as I was too high to drive, but I persuaded him to carry on (the test was looming). After an hour of concentration, I wilted. My euphoria evaporated and I could barely keep the wheel straight, so the lesson was shortened. Whilst I have had a lot of precious experiences in my career, there is nothing that compares with the raw emotion and sheer exhilaration during a first delivery. I would not have missed it for the world.

After the dental operation, I was afraid of being off sick for too long, so I returned to work after two weeks, knowing that I had to go back for another operation. This was scheduled for the holidays, so that I did not accrue any more sick-leave, which would have extended the course. For weeks, I was only able to eat soft foods, and lived on a diet of weetabix, banana, boiled eggs and mince and mash. Also, I could not stand coffee for weeks, and drank gallons of cocoa. Just as I was beginning to eat more solid food, I went back in for the second operation. So I had a soft diet again. The advantage was that I lost nearly a stone in weight - not a recommended dietary method, though. By the time I had the second operation, it was time to go on Community. Here we were based with a community midwife, to learn her role, and gain experience of community midwifery. Because 'A' and I did not have transport, we had to live in the nurses home, even though we were married, and men were not allowed in the bedrooms - only the lounge area. Jim did not bother visiting at all, but waited for me to come home.

We got the worst three months of the year - over Christmas and New Year and the bad weather. The four of us were split into two, and we worked with different teams of midwives. During this time on community we visited Mums after they had delivered their babies, and sometimes ante-natal Mums. We were on call quite a lot, and even though we had been working all day we could be called out at anytime in the night. The hospital was quite innovative in those days in that they had a Domino scheme. Domino stood for <u>Dom</u>icilary <u>In</u> <u>Out</u>. The mother booked as if for a home delivery. Just prior to the birth, she went into hospital with the domicilary or district midwife, who delivered her in hospital. Then mother and baby would be transferred home again after about six hours. This had the advantages of being a hospital birth, in case of mishaps but with the Mum hardly being away from home. Often the Mum could put the other children to bed, go in hospital, have the baby and be home again before the children woke up in the morning.

Whilst we were on Community the midwives decided that they would stick to the rota as usual during Christmas and New Year. We both said that was fair, but when I looked at the off-duty I was disappointed. Christmas Day was on a Wednesday. The other students' off-duty for that week was early finish Tuesday (1.30 pm), Christmas Day and Boxing Day off and late start on the 27th December. As she was off-duty all that time, it meant that I was on duty and living in at the nurses' home alone. As a major concession, I was allowed to go home for the day on Christmas Day but only because I was on the phone and lived near the hospital. Needless to say Jim and I had a miserable Christmas that year. The off-duty worked against me for the New Year as well, and I was on call all New Year. The other student was not complaining though, she got brilliant off-duty. But she didn't get a home delivery or a New Year's Day baby either, so it was worth it, after all.

The home birth took place on New Year's Eve, and I was quite pleased when I was called out at midnight. Jim wasn't too pleased though, for in my excitement, I was late ringing him to wish him 'Happy New Year'. There was always a race to be able to deliver the first Christmas baby and the first New Year baby. The Mum already had a young toddler, and everything had progressed normally during this pregnancy. The Midwife on call knew how excited I was at having a home delivery. Mum had the baby around 3 am, but he was only very tiny. He was crying all right but, because of his size, we had to take him to the Special Care Baby Unit (SCBU). On the way through Delivery to go up to SCBU, I saw a midwife and shouted in passing, "have I got the New Year baby?" But I was pipped to the post, there had been a hospital delivery at 1.30 am. Never mind, at least I had experienced a home birth. The little boy romped on once he was in SCBU and the nurses could not fill him. He gained weight quickly and soon went home.

I was attached to one main midwife and I spent most of the time with her. She taught me an awful lot, not only about midwifery, but about the differences in nursing patients when you were a guest in their house, which was so different from the ward. Usually I followed her off-duty, but sometimes I worked with other midwives who gave me a different view and a wider experience of approaches.

One of the team was a born comedian, and had me in stitches with her gentle humour, and twinkling eyes. Whilst on the district, offers of cups of tea are a variable feast. You either get one offered at every house and became water-logged and desperately need a loo, or no-one offers you a drink in four hours. This particular day, we had not had a drink all morning, and we were 'gagging for a brew' as they say in Lancashire. At the next house, the midwife started trying hints. "Is that the kettle I hear boiling?" she asked innocently. "Yes," replied the Mum. "You know what we want" said the midwife. "Oh yes," said the Mum with a knowing look as she went back to the kitchen. The midwife winked at me, and I smiled back in anticipation. The Mum returned with a little dish with hot water in and some cotton wool balls, so that we could bathe the baby's eyes. We looked at each other - mouths wide open, and then we both laughed. The Mum looked perplexed so the midwife explained what we really wanted. It was so embarrassing. The Mum made us a drink, and we all laughed again. For the next few days, the midwives were always pressured to have a brew at that house! As it happened the midwives complained about me because I did not drink tea. They said no decent midwife didn't like tea, but I learned to live with it (or without it, as far as tea goes).

Following the three months on Community we were allowed back into Hospital again to learn about abnormal midwifery. During this period Cynthia was expecting her second child, and as usual things were not progressing well. During pregnancies,

Cynthia's blood pressure soars, and she ends up being admitted to Hospital. Because she had a toddler, she decided to have a Domino delivery for her second child. When she went into labour, I was actually working a late shift on delivery, but Cynthia was with the Community Midwives. However, the staff were very lenient with me and let me keep popping in. I was not really fit for work that day, so they only gave me small jobs to do. Then an admission came in and I was sent round to the admissions suite to deal with the new patient.

By the time I got back an hour later, Cynthia had delivered her second daughter, Elaine. Unbeknown to me, things had been going wrong with her labour. The GP had been called in and her care had been transferred to the Obstetrician and Hospital Midwives because the baby's heart beat was dropping. After giving Cynthia oxygen things got better and Elaine arrived. They had deliberately sent me out of the way just in case. Afterwards, I was even less fit for work, I was so happy to be an Aunty again. It was decided that I could look after Cynthia and Elaine for the rest of my shift, and then accompany her home in the ambulance after the birth. I had a lovely day, and soon after the birth Cynthia decided she was starving. It was past teatime, so I went all round the wards trying to scrounge a meal for her. I managed to get a cheese salad, which she was delighted with then promptly left. Humph, after all my effort, Sisters! But I forgave her, because she drank copious cups of tea and gave me the highest accolade, "to say you don't drink tea yourself, kid, you make a brilliant cup of tea."

Sadly, not all labours had a happy ending. Sometimes babies were stillborn, or birth defects were found. These could be minor or major, but all had the same effect on the mothers, who fretted about any detail of their baby that was less than perfect. Other children were acutely ill at birth and needed skilled and careful handling, or surgery for them to survive. If the child needed surgery, it usually had to go to the Regional Baby Unit - twenty-eight miles away. In those days, mothers were often left behind in the peripheral Hospital, worrying about their babies from afar, and not being able to touch and cuddle them. Jim's sister was in that situation. Her little girl had a perforated appendix at a few hours old, which is exceptionally rare so young. The baby was whisked off to the Regional Unit and Mum was not allowed to go. On the second day, she signed her own discharge against medical advice so that she could go and stay with the baby. As a professional, I felt I ought to persuade her to stay in hospital, but as a sister-in-law, I did not blame her and felt the ruling was wrong. This situation is much better nowadays as mothers are positively encouraged to go with their babies on transfer to other hospitals.

Some babies were born with a life-long diagnosis such as Down's Syndrome. Occasionally grossly abnormal babies were born. Sometimes ladies would be admitted with a threatened abortion or miscarriage. The words abortion and miscarriage actually mean the same - a premature ending of pregnancy. But Mums do not see it that way. If you asked if they had had an abortion, they would be offended, but not if you asked about miscarriages. A threatened abortion is often nature's way of saying there is something wrong with the pregnancy, or that something may be wrong with the baby. I decided that if I was ever in the position of having a threatened abortion, I would not try and 'save' it, but let nature take its course. But first I had to get pregnant, and that was something that was banned during my training!

The two years of training were coming to a close and the dreaded exam loomed near. The exam had three components. Firstly you had to write two case studies about ladies whose babies you had delivered. My first attempt was given back to me as being suitable for Woman's Own magazine. Well, it was the first time I had ever done a case-study, so I had to learn, didn't I? As well as the case studies we had a written exam and then an oral examination. The nearest exam centre for us was thirty-five miles away. The exam and the oral were on two different days, so it entailed two trips over the Pennines.

The exam was held in the nurses' home in the large ballroom of a hospital. It was a scorching hot day, and all the windows were wide open. Unfortunately, someone was playing music, some students were watching a video in a classroom nearby and the traffic noises were so loud that it made concentration very difficult. We did complain, but it did not improve very much. The questions were fairly straight forward, but there is always the worry that you have missed something or read the question wrongly. The weekly tests now came in handy, as it was much easier to get your thoughts together quickly under exam conditions after two years of tests.

Once the exam is over, you hope that you have passed. You know you have done your best, but you can only remember what you have missed out, or that you ran out of time. Then comes the dreaded post-mortem. All the other students start asking what you put for question three. The more answers you hear, the worse it gets. People mention bits that you have missed out, or you realise that you have interpreted the question in a totally different way. By now, you are convinced that you have failed miserably. For the next few weeks, you swing between easily passed, scraped through and abject failure. Sailing through or getting distinctions are unimportant. All you want is the pass-mark.

As if the written exam was not enough, you had the worry of your oral exam hanging over you. This exam counts as one of the ten worst experiences in my life. We had all gone in a minibus this time, to save travelling costs. The orals were twenty minutes long and spread out over the whole day. There were three examiners, two Midwives and a Consultant. By the time of the oral, they had read your case-studies and your exam papers. When being prepared for your oral, you were told that they could ask you anything from the case studies and exam, or anything else they wanted. You were warned that you could carelessly lead your oral into areas that you were not comfortable with. Thus, you were afraid of saying very much at all.

The whole day revolved round bells. The bell rang and the person being interviewed had to stop speaking immediately, get up and walk away. Then the next person came in. This procedure was drummed into you, so that the orals did not over-run. The bell rang and I walked across the large room that had several desks spread around the outside. I gave my candidate number to the examiners and sat down nervously. The two Midwives were lovely and welcoming, but the Consultant was more difficult. He gave no eye contact and was doodling on his pad. He asked some very nit-picking little questions, making me feel very disgruntled, unsure, and with a feeling that I was portraying myself in a bad light.

At last, the blissful bell rang in the room. The Consultant had just started to speak but I jumped up ready to leave, according to the instructions. The Obstetrician stopped me and said he had not finished with me, and I had to answer him one final question. "Do you want to walk out of here and never come back?" he asked. I could not believe it and stared at him. All the other candidates had left and the new ones were entering. "Well, come on" he said "answer me." "Yes," I squeaked in reply. He laughed at me "Well go on then, get going," he said. I ran out of the room, getting dirty looks from the organisers. I was almost in tears when I found another student in the corridor. I blurted out how awful he had been, that I did not know whether I had done all right or failed miserably. I told her about the doodling and she laughed. "Oh, we had the same examiner. Not only did he doodle all the way through the exam, he drew a picture of me, then turned the pad round so that I could recognise myself!"

Those of us who had been examined in the morning, then went for a leisurely lunch, and a look at the shops before returning in the mini-bus. We did not have long to wait for the results, the oral often merely confirming the results of the case studies and written exams. The fateful day arrived. I was fortunate, my postman arrives at 7.10 am, so I got my results very early. With trembling hands I opened the letter to read that I had passed. No, I thought hurriedly, read it again, you might have made a mistake. The postman was walking back up the street, so I asked him to read it just in case. He confirmed that I had passed, and congratulated me. WOW, I was a State Certified Midwife. (Certified being the operative word to my friends and family). I was ecstatic, but it was a little early to start ringing round. Also, it is always difficult to ring peers in case they have not passed. I rang Mum and Cynthia and then at 8.00 am, I rang the School of Midwifery. They were delighted that I had passed, as I was the first to ring. The next news was not as good as the next few results were all failures. Our own little group had passed, but it took the joy out of passing to know that other colleagues were suffering.

But nevertheless, I had passed and I went to pay the exorbitant registration fee to the Central Midwives Board (CMB) so that I could go on their register. Eventually I got my State badge from the CMB, with my registration number on the back. It was important that we knew our number as we had to put it on the form each time we delivered a baby.

Towards the end of our training, we were asked if we wanted jobs on the Maternity Unit, and I said yes. I went to the Sewing Room to be measured for my new pale blue staff midwives' uniform. These were old fashioned button through dresses, with collar studs for buttons, and a tight plastic collar that rubbed your neck mercilessly. Added to that was a white pinny, blue belt, little frilly cuffs, and a Sisters' hat. Sisters' hats were worn by staff midwives to show that they were midwives, rather than general nurses. They were of a softer fabric with silky spots on - far more glamorous than the pale blue stripe. Whilst pinnies had been essential attire during Cynthia's day, they were hardly ever worn by 1974, except for some strange reason, when working on ante-natal clinic. With my new uniform ready, I started a new phase of my life as a Staff Midwife.

CHAPTER FOUR

FURTHER TRAINING

My new job as a staff midwife was a little like going through training again. We were not allocated to a specific ward, but had to go to each area on rotation during our first year, so that we were familiar with the whole unit. We also had to do three months nights each year.

Suddenly life has changed. You do not feel any different, but by donning a different colour of dress, everybody treats you differently. Doctors actually talk to you, Consultants even speak. When you answer the 'phone, people will actually give you a message instead of asking for the person in charge. It does not matter how trivial the message may be, people will not pass messages on to mere students. But the down-side of this is that no longer can you say, "I don't know, I'll go and ask Sister." Eventually, the buck stops with you if Sister is on a day off. Decision-making becomes an important part of life as a staff nurse. The week after qualifying, you are allowed back into school to learn about management and legal issues for two days - the staff nurse's induction block. But we did not qualify at the same time as the general students, so we did not get to go to school for about two months. By then, we had learnt to sink or swim.

My first place of work was on SCBU. I really loved it there. All those tiny babies that could fit in your hand. They were so vulnerable and technology had not advanced very far by the mid seventies. The smallest baby that had survived had been 1lb 10ozs and that was seen as a major breakthrough by the medical and nursing team, as she had been born at twenty-eight weeks of pregnancy. She was such a fighter, right from the word go. But then girls always fare better. No, this is not a sexist remark, but is a proven fact.

After I had been qualified a couple of weeks, the Senior Nursing Officer came on her daily tour. "Good morning nurse," she said, "Congratulations on passing your exam and do you know you are going on night duty?" No, I have not missed any punctuation marks out, it was all said in one breath! As this was November, my heart sank. I would be on nights at Christmas. Last Christmas had been disastrous because of Community, and this year I would be on nights, too. Also, the other worrying thought was that you often did night duty at the same time each year, so I could end up being on nights every Christmas, and through the winter months. Full-time night duty was hard work in winter as you went to work and came home in the dark, and slept throughout daylight hours. The one advantage I had was that I slept like a log during the day, and my digestion was not upset by eating breakfast at 7.00 pm and lunch at midnight.

Because I coped well with nights, I opted to do straight weeks of nights - eight nights on duty consecutively and then six nights off. This way, you made sure that you got alternate weekends off, and you could predict your off duty time. The poor unfortunates who could not or would not work long stretches got appalling off duty, such as three on, two off, five on, one off, two on, three off and so on. Really it made them even worse, because their body clocks never caught up. Holidays were also extended by a week if you had three nights off prior to your holiday and three nights off afterwards. The other advantage of doing a long stretch was that you stayed on the same ward for eight nights. If you were only in for a short stretch, you were on a different ward practically every night, which was very disjointing. On the same ward, you managed to build up a rapport with the Mums and babies, who usually stayed in six days for a normal birth and ten days for a Caesarean Section. By previous arrangement, Mums having a second baby could go home after forty-eight hours, to the care of the District Midwife.

And so I went on nights, a fairly newly qualified midwife, with a lot to learn. Being on nights meant taking my turn in working on delivery suite. On the 23rd of December, I had been talking to the senior midwife on duty and saying that I had not had a delivery on my own since qualifying. She promised me one for the next shift. Once you qualify, it is pretty hard to get a delivery, because the next group of students or, even worse, medical students, are all fighting to have the deliveries. I came on duty the next night, Christmas Eve. Sister remembered and promised that the first patient that came in could be mine.

We already had two patients in, but sadly they were both having spontaneous abortions. I reflected sadly how those ladies must be feeling. The loss of a baby at anytime is overwhelming and soul destroying but to lose one at Christmas, when all the world is celebrating the birth of the Infant Jesus, must be doubly painful.

The delivery suite settled down for the night. Patients comfortable, supplies stocked up, equipment checked, drugs checked. Delivery suites tend to be like that. All or nothing. There never seems to be a happy medium where you can go from one patient to the next in a leisurely fashion. They all arrive together, and then somebody else wants 'to push now.' Sometimes you have to be good at running, and you could certainly do with skates on at times.

The phone rang at about 10.30 pm. When I answered the phone, a lady rang to say that she was in labour and she was coming in. "Oh, goody," I said, "I will be looking after you, and there is a strong possibility that you could be the Christmas Day baby." I took her details and she rang off. I went to the records office and got her notes out. This was her second baby and the pregnancy had been uneventful. Her first delivery had been 'normal' as well, so I knew she would be my patient. I got all the paperwork ready, and prepared a room for her. But she did not come. Midnight came, and still no lady. Christmas greetings were given to each other as Christmas Day began. The front door bell rang. I jumped up to answer it, saying "this will be my patient." I was wrong. It was the local taxi-drivers dropping a big teddy bear off to be given to the Christmas Day baby. I told them that we would make sure it was passed on to the first new Mum and baby of the day. Whilst I was thanking them profusely, they went off into the night, too embarrassed for thanks, but glad to share the Christmas spirit.

For Christmas Day, I had knitted all the little premature babies on SCBU a matinee jacket. As I had a couple spare, I had decided I would give one to the Christmas baby, so it now had two presents waiting. But where was my patient? I paced the unit, wondering what had happened. At about 1.45 am, the phone rang again. It was my patient. "What happened?" I asked. She laughed, "As soon as I rang you, the pains stopped, but they're back with a vengeance now. I'm coming in." Within twenty minutes she arrived with her husband and a sleepy toddler. Dad decided not to stay for the birth, and took the little boy home. Whilst more Dads were staying to watch the birth in the mid seventies, it was not as common as it is now. We quickly built up a rapport as I examined her. Her pains were coming about five minutes apart, were quite strong and lasting. The neck of her womb was also opening up, so everything was progressing nicely. I explained about the race for the Christmas baby and she laughingly said she would try and have the baby by 8.00 am before I went off duty. "Well, could you make it 7.30 am." I replied, "because I will have all the paper work to do." She started to laugh again, and said she would try her best, but then another pain started, and the laughs ceased.

When she eventually delivered the baby, she did not ask the usual two questions, What is it? Is it all right? She asked "What time is it Linda?" "Twenty past six," I replied, "and you have got a lovely baby girl." Oh dear, was I so obvious? Was she so worried about the time? Well, I will never know that, but I bet it helped her push the baby out! I said goodbye as mum and babe went to the ward, complete with presents. Later in the day, they both had their pictures taken for the local paper, and because of the time of year, mum and babe went home early to join the rest of the family. A precious night for me too, I mused as my head hit the pillow. Years later, I was able to use this experience in an article when the nursing press asked for humorous stories about Christmas in a Delivery Suite.

Back on days, life was much more hectic. I was put on a ward for three months. Soon after I arrived on the ward, rotation moved most of the senior staff off, and I became more senior fairly quickly. The senior sister, helped me a great deal, but often she handed the ward over to me and then went on her days off, leaving another Midwife and me to run the ward. On days, there was a lot more going on, and decisions often had to be made. Usually, when the senior sister came back from her days off, I had a list of queries for her. Did I do right in this situation? Did you know that such a thing has happened? There is a change to this rule, etc. etc. Nowadays there is a system of preceptorship for newly qualified staff. A preceptor is appointed who looks after you for the first four to six months after qualifying. You discuss things together at length, and it makes for wiser decision making and management. It's a good system, and was carried out informally in the seventies, but was only as good as the person you worked with. I was fortunate that I got a lot of help.

Also, with rotation, I kept bumping into my 'special midwife' again.

The ward was a mixed ward where both ante-natal and post-natal patients were nursed. The majority of patients were post-natal, but there were always some patients who were having problems with their pregnancy and were admitted for rest or investigations. One of the serious complications of pregnancy is called pre-eclampsia. It used to be called toxaemia but as no toxins have been found in the blood stream, it is now called pre-eclampsia, although the word toxaemia is still heard sometimes. With pre-eclampsia, the mother develops high blood pressure, becomes swollen or waterlogged (called oedema) and has protein present in the urine. Midwives are constantly watching out for pre-eclampsia, so urine, weight and blood pressure are checked at every visit. The only treatment is for the lady to rest. This is virtually impossible at home, especially if there are other children, so often it is better to admit the mother to hospital for an enforced rest. Trouble is, lying in a hospital bed does not encourage the mother to rest. She frets and fumes about what she could be doing or what is actually going on at home. I used to think bed rest in hospital was counter-productive for some ladies, whose worrying outdid their resting. The problems also affect the family. Little children become upset when Mum is not around, and some Dads cannot cope.

At the end of my three months on the ward, I became a patient again. This time to have investigations as to why I was not conceiving. I wanted to get on with having a family now I was qualified but nothing was happening. I was back on night duty again and the Consultant said he would leave me a letter about my results on the Delivery Suite. I came on duty and picked the letter up from the office as I reported on night-duty. As I had forgotten there would be a letter for me, I opened it whilst sharing a joke with the girls. My face slipped as I read the letter, and I hurried out to the toilet. The letter said quite plainly that I would not be having any children. I was devastated but had to go to the ward to begin my shift. When the day staff had gone, my 'special midwife' came to me. She had watched my face when I read the letter. I showed her the letter, glad that I had her there with me.

That night I worked on automatic pilot. I had an auxiliary nurse on duty with me, whom I had not met before, so I did not feel I could tell her what the matter was. I do not know what she thought of me, as I was poor company that night. My 'special midwife' came every hour to check on me and spent her meal break with me. She was brilliant. I do not think I would have got through without her. This news made me feel very differently about my career. A career was only something to do until I had babies, and then put on hold until they had grown up. I was not ambitious, and could have been quite happy staying a Staff Midwife, but I now had thirty-five years to work. I had to do some serious thinking about my long term career plans, even if it was only to take my mind off being childless. There had been murmuring in the nursing profession that a direct entry midwife was a sort of second class midwife and they should really have their general training as well. With the two issues happening at the same time, I had to re-think my long term plans. Very reluctantly, I went to the general school to see about undertaking further training. I saw a tutor and he gave me an informal interview. He agreed to accept me as a student nurse, on a shortened course. During my student nurse training, I would still receive my Staff Midwifes pay, but all increments would be frozen until a year after I qualified again.

I was joined on the course by another direct entry midwife, 'B' who was just qualifying and wanted to go straight on to general training. We already knew each other from the Maternity Unit, so we had a head start. We had to do two and a half years of training instead of three, which annoyed us. Two other post-registration students also joined the group who had qualified as Mental Health nurses and they only had to train for 18 months to become general nurses. We felt that was totally unfair as we had been looking after seriously ill patients, who had had operations, and sick babies. We were used to drips, blood transfusions, unconscious patients and others. The Mental Health nurses had many other different skills, but had not looked after acutely ill patients like us.

We joined the AA group which had a large number of men, and older married women in the group. As 'B' and I had done the introductory block and medicine block, we started in a surgical theory block of four weeks. Then it was back to the wards. The time in school flew by, and we were a lively crowd - none livelier than 'B' and I. I have never been known for my reticence, shyness or loss of words, why say one word when twenty will do, I always say. It's a hereditary condition that all my family have - verbal diarrhoea! On my own I am a chatty, talkative extrovert, but manageable (usually.) But she was very similar. Together we were dynamite and were forever giggling and laughing. We were soon in trouble with the nurse tutors, who were forever telling us off. (Hope my students don't read this!) In the end, we wrote notes to each other, rather than talking, but we could not always contain the giggles.

Another problem I had in school was that I always yawn a lot, but the tutors assumed I was bored, and one even suggested that I leave the class. Now, I don't know about you, but if I have been told not to do anything like yawning, I want to yawn all the more. Oops, there I go, yawning again, just because I am typing about it! But it certainly caused me problems in school.

On my first ward, I had to become used to the white dress and being called student again. The first few times somebody shouted 'staff', I must admit that I turned my head, momentarily forgetting. But the advantages far outweighed the disadvantages. It was lovely to have no ultimate responsibility. If anyone asked me a difficult question, I would smile sweetly and say "I will have to ask Sister or Staff." And yet I was getting the salary of a staff nurse. The best of both worlds. In the sixties they would have had to go back to student nurse pay during a second training, which discouraged many. That ruling had changed fairly recently, and I was glad that I was able to benefit from it.

Although by now I had passed my driving test, we could not afford a car. I had bought a Honda motorbike to get myself around. If Jim saw me coming on the bike, he pretended he did not know me. It took me a while to get used to it, but once I did, I was never at home and really loved the freedom it gave me. I had always hated buses and was a little travel sick still on long journeys. Just to prove travel sickness is psychological, I have never, ever been sick whilst driving. Yet I cannot go very far by bus or car as a passenger. Trains, boats and planes are fine.

One Sunday afternoon I was going back to work on a split shift and was travelling up the main road to the hospital. I approached a cross-road but was on the main road. I saw a woman in a car approaching the cross-road, who looked straight at me, then pulled out across my path and knocked me off my bike. Fortunately, I just missed going through a plate glass window. The lady jumped out of the car and apologised saying, "I never saw you." I could not believe that, I was wearing a shocking orange wet suit! She cried out "oh, my husband will kill me, he's a policeman." Then she noticed my uniform "oh no," she said "my twin sister is a nurse." She told me her sister's name and I said I knew her. That added to her embarrassment. Thankfully she admitted liability, and we exchanged addresses. I picked my bike up and fortunately it was still rideable. I was worried about being late back for work. I hurried into work and blurted an apology to the ward sister, explaining why I was late. She looked at my bruised and cut arms and legs and made me have a drink in the kitchen. Shortly afterwards I started work, but fairly quickly, I began to shake. I was experiencing delayed shock. I do not know whether it is the nurse training, but I always cope at the time of a disaster and then go to pieces later when it's all over. Sister took one look at me and sent me home. Jim was delighted when I arrived home early, until he heard what had happened. He was very upset, and ranted and raved a bit. That is Jim's way of coping. Shout first then ask questions later! As it happened, this was the first in a long line of bi-annual crashes, which started in 1976 and progressed up to and including 1998. But some of these crashes are part of the story, so I will not expand now.

After three months on the medical ward, we went back into school for another block of study, before going on to a surgical ward. I went back to the surgical ward. One of the doctors whom I had worked with on the maternity ward was now working on the Gynae team of doctors. He was most put out that I was back in students uniform and insisted on calling me 'staff.' Because of my midwifery experience, I always got the Gynae patients. And that included the shaves. But I never repeated my earlier mistake and shaved the wrong bit!

On a surgical ward, life was spent running up and down to theatre. The theatre porter would arrive with a label with the required patient's name on it. The person in charge would check the patient that was going to theatre, and you would then dash off to theatre trying to keep up with the trolley and the patient. The patient might often be very distressed and frightened at this time. It was very difficult to reassure them, whilst running at what felt like a hundred miles per hour.

In the theatre, most patients wanted the ward nurse to stay with them until they were anaesthetised. Having been a patient, I knew how reassuring it was to have a familiar face around. It depended on the individual anaesthetist or nurse as to whether you were allowed to stay or not. Sometimes you were curtly dismissed before you had hardly got over the theatre threshold. If something was happening elsewhere, you could get left waiting in the anaesthetic room, until you were allowed to go. The patients got even more upset if there was a long wait in the anaesthetic room. Also, you knew that when you got back to the ward, you would be in trouble with Sister for staying too long. It was a no win situation. Sometimes I would dig my heels in and insist on staying with a patient who was nervous and had asked me to stay until they were asleep. I was usually met with dirty looks from the doctor or nurse. But a promise is a promise, and I would ignore them. Nowadays, this is called advocacy, but we did not call it that in the seventies. It was working on your gut feelings for what felt right for the patient. Gut feelings are not taught in the nursing curriculum, but it is something you learn with experience. Sometimes, you cannot explain why you have a gut feeling about a patient, but it often turns out to be right.

The journey back from theatre was even worse. The theatre would ring to say that the patient was ready. You had to drop what you were doing, scurry up there to collect your patient, ensuring in the meantime that the bed had been remade with clean linen to receive the patient. In reality, when the theatre rang, they were probably just starting to sew the patient up, but they did not want the theatre list held up. Far better that you should stand there twiddling your thumbs waiting for your patient, rather than their work be delayed. When the patient came out of theatre, and showed the slightest sign of coming round, you were allowed to take the patient back to the ward. Only the major operations went to a recovery ward for a day or two for more intensive care. Often the patients still had an airway in to stop them from choking. The patient's chin also had to be held to prevent them choking. Thus the run back to the ward would begin with you hoping and praying that nothing untoward would happen. Some patients were quite violent. It was very difficult trying to run holding the trolley, and the patient's chin and steer round corners all at the same time. It was always a relief to get back to the ward where there was piped suction and oxygen on the walls, and plenty of senior nurses to help you. Thank God it has long since changed. No patient is ever allowed out of theatre before their airway is removed. They go to a special recovery area, until they are fully recovered. Although you still have to be vigilant on the way back to the ward, there is not the panicky feeling that there used to be, with an unconscious patient.

After finishing on the surgical ward it was back to the school for another theory block. When we were in school we always went to the hospital canteen for meals. One day, a group of us were walking through the grounds when a lady hurried up to us. She had the most enormous braces on her teeth. With great difficulty, she said, "excuse me, could you tell me the way to the dental clinic?" I felt so sorry for her. "Of course I can," I replied. "It's

across here, into the main building there, along the corridor......
Oh it's easier to take you part of the way than explain it.   I'm
going that way." The lady looked irritatedly at her watch, and
said, "I will be late for the clinic." I smiled at her, trying to put
her at her ease, "Oh, don't worry about being late, they are never
on time, you always have to wait hours for the dentist,"   I
replied.   "I am the dentist" she said. Oh no. Oh what a big
mouth I was. Oh why didn't the ground open up and swallow
me. I apologised to her immediately. She replied that it was all
right, but looked very embarrassed. I quickly directed her to the
clinic and slunk off in the opposite direction. My friends just
stared, and could not believe what had happened. It was one of
the most embarrassing experiences of my life, but not quite the
worst. One of my colleagues says I should tell about my worst
one, but it is just a little too embarrassing.

Whilst we were in this theory block, we were learning about
orthopaedic nursing (bones) and accident and emergency
nursing before going onto those wards. There were several new
skills to be learnt such as bandaging, and applying plaster of
paris (POP). I made the mistake of wearing a sleeveless dress
that day, so I ended up being the patient. Plaster of paris used to
be delivered in rolls of plaster-encrusted mesh. When you are
wanting to apply a POP, you wet the roll and then quickly apply
it to the injured limb. It is a real art to watch, and takes a great
deal of skill. Another student started applying the plaster to my
arm quickly before it set. At first it just felt warm and wet, but
as it dried, it became very uncomfortable. "It feels tight," I said.
Everybody laughed. "Am I supposed to be getting pins and

needles in my hands?" I asked. "Oh, isn't she a comic?" one of my friends said, thinking I was joking. By now, I was feeling distinctly faint. "Should my hand be going blue?" I croaked. The tutor ran across the room "Oh dear," she said, "she's serious," and quickly got the shears to cut the plaster off. What a relief when it was removed. After that, I always made certain that plasters were comfortable for patients. Nowadays, 'fibreglass plasters' are applied, and are available in many colours. The local boys are so proud to have a POP made in the local football team colours.

'B' and I went onto orthopaedic wards first. We were to spend one week on days to learn about the ward and then onto nights for six weeks, before rounding off with a final week of days. When we went on nights, we were down at the other hospital, a mile down the road from the main one. The main hospital had been the old workhouse, built on what was then the outskirts of town. The hospital we went to for night duty had been built by public subscription by the local people, plus some generous philanthropists. It was felt to be a far superior hospital than the main one. At one stage, nurses would be trained completely separately. There was quite a bit of snobbery attached to it. By the time I trained, all training was done at the main one so there was no schism, but there were still lots of senior staff who held the attitude.

The other hospital did not have canteen facilities at night, which was a shame because the meals there were lovely. At night, you could order meals, but they were plated up during the day, and put in a cabinet to be warmed up later, in what was like a forerunner of a modern microwave. They were not nice meals. Because of this, the kitchen provided unlimited toast, jam and marmalade. Most of us lived on toast for the entire spell of night duty. I never complained. I loved toast, and it was free, but some moaned. At the main hospital, the canteen was open at night because it was a bigger hospital.

When we first went on nights, we were second years and there were a lot of finalists working with us. After one week, the finalists got their results and all moved back onto days. Suddenly, 'B' and I were the most senior people on nights, after having been mere juniors the week before. It was an astonishing and rapid change. As the hospital was now short of students, we were put on the Gynae wards, working opposite nights to each other, because they found out that we were qualified midwives. On my shifts, I was alone on the ward, with no other nurse to support me. It's eerie to spend a whole night alone. You hear every creak, groan, moan and weirder sounds and your mind runs riot. The only time you got off the ward was for your meal break, and it was a precious time to talk to others, to keep you sane. It was a good chance to do some studying, but the problem was that the minute you got your books out, your eyelids started drooping. Knitting was a far better occupation to keep you awake, but oh the noise if you dropped a knitting needle. The sound was magnified a million times at night.

Back on days, I went back to the orthopaedic ward, but as I had done most of my nights on Gynae, I had not learned very much. To this day I remain vague about orthopaedic nursing.

My next stint was in the Accident and Emergency Department (A&E Dept). I quite enjoyed the experience here. You never knew what was going to happen next, or be brought through the door. As with Delivery Suite, it was usually all or nothing. One week, I worked in the Fracture Clinic with a Charge Nurse. When there was no clinic I went into the A&E Dept, but if anything interesting came along, he would come and find me. One day he came to the door of the A&E Dept and mouthed across the room to me. I thought he said "I'm going for a cup of tea." Always being ready for a brew, I asked "can I come and help you?" When I saw the shocked and disgusted look on his face, I realised I had said the wrong thing. He had said 'I'm going for a pee!' Oh what a red face I had. Especially as the story went the rounds for days.

Because people knew I was a midwife and nursery nurse, I was given all the children and Gynae patients to look after. I had already started enquiring about going on to do Children's training after qualifying as a general nurse. I had been swept along by a friend at Church, who had decided to go and do her Children's training. I had also been back on the children's surgical ward. I loved that ward. It combined my two favourite things - nursing and children. Children's nursing was even better than midwifery and once I had qualified as a general nurse I would be able to do extra training. It would involve going to a children's hospital twenty-five miles away, which would bring its own problems, as I still only had my bike.

On Easter Sunday, I was working an early shift. I was feeling a bit miffed that I was having to work on Easter Sunday. I looked at the clock, and realised that the Church service would just be starting. I then started thinking about my career. Could I really stand doing another training? I had not even finished this one yet. Sister called to me and brought me back to earth with a bump. "We've had a message from the ambulance service, they're bringing a very poorly baby in who's had a fit and sounds like he has got meningitis. Would you like to help?" I got the emergency room ready just in time. Assisting the doctor, we got the patient stable and then I was left looking after the child until the ambulance came to transfer him to the Isolation Hospital children's ward, further up the hill. I stayed with the baby, taking him in the ambulance and handed him over to the nurses. All the time I was looking after him, I found I had a terrific sense of peace. Everyone else was running around but I just quietly got on with looking after the little boy. I knew then that this was the career for me. I would not go back to midwifery, but become a children's nurse.

However, before that, I had to pass my general training! My training lasted a hundred and twenty six weeks. At the start of it, I wrote all the numbers from a hundred and twenty six down to one on a chart and crossed a week off every Monday. At first, the numbers did not feel to be moving much, but very soon, time was hurtling towards another exam. But there were other specialities to be experienced first.

I went on a medical ward again, and experienced something that is the fear of all practising nurses. A drug error. A colleague and I had been giving all the medicines out when we realised we had given too strong a dose of a heart tablet. The patient swallowed the tablet, and then asked about it. Oh horrors! We locked the drug trolley and hurried off to the sluice. What should we do? Tell and face the consequence or keep quiet and hope nothing would happen? We were both too honest not to tell, so we went miserably to see the Sister.

It was action stations straightaway. The Doctor was summoned to examine the patient and write in the notes and the Nursing Officer was sent for to deal with us. Oh what a roasting we got. It is bad enough that you have made a mistake without a telling off. But telling off we got in no uncertain terms. She told us off together and then rounded on me to say that I should have known better, because I was already a qualified nurse. My head sank even lower on my chest. It was agony. At last she dismissed us from her presence and as we were going through the door she said, "can I say that I admire your honesty and courage for telling the truth." A small shred of comfort, at a time when you felt that you were not fit to be a nurse any longer. Whilst it is not something I would advocate trying, you only ever make one drug error in your whole career. You are so neurotically careful for evermore. And the patient? Yes, the patient never ailed a thing, thank God.

This ward was below the children's medical ward. There was an outdoor play area at the back of the ward, so it was an added bonus on this ward to watch the children playing outside during a quiet afternoon.

Back into School again, and this time the theory was to prepare us for working in the Operating Theatre. I looked forward to this venture as I had enjoyed the time I had spent in the Maternity Unit Theatre previously. The first operation that was on the Gynae list was investigating why a woman could not conceive, and it was the same surgeon who had operated on me. "Aren't you glad you didn't watch this before your operation?" he asked, and I agreed.

The second operation was a termination of pregnancy. I had deliberated long and hard about watching a termination. For myself, I did not believe in abortion, and would not assist at one, but I may still have to nurse them on the ward, and patients might ask me what happens. So I decided I would watch just one. The very same doctors who had tried to help the first lady conceive, were now taking away a normal baby out of someone else. My heart started pounding and I started to become upset. 'Why could they not take this baby out and transplant it into the first lady? Then everybody would be happy,' I started thinking, totally illogically. Enough was enough. I decided I had made a wrong decision and sneaked out the back of the theatre into a large cupboard to cry. When I did not come out, a theatre technician shouted, "Are you all right?" before he realised I was bawling my head off. Very embarrassed, he guided me into the staff room and brought Sister, before he scooted back to theatre.

A cup of coffee and a box of tissues appeared. Sister talked about my feelings and I alternately talked and sobbed incoherently. Eventually she sent for one of the girls out of my group, who she thought might be more helpful. When she arrived, the bawling started again. I got through a lot of coffee and tissues that day, and Sister sent me home early. When I came in the next day, Sister announced to all the staff "Nurse Sawley is banned from Gynae Theatre from now on, as we haven't time to keep mopping the floor between cases." Did I really cry that much?

As a third year student, I was now gaining more responsibility and learning new skills. Third years wore red belts - red for danger I suppose. The training was not dragging at all now, and we seemed to be rushing towards June 4th, our state final examination day. Another placement was spent on a care of the elderly ward or geriatrics as it used to be called. I loved my time on this unit, and although it was hard manual work, the time passed very quickly, and I enjoyed talking to the elderly patients. They were so interesting and had so much to tell you about their lives. I even nursed a couple of people who had worked at the family cotton mill, and they remembered Dad and talked about him with fond memories.

My next to the last placement should have been back on an adult medical ward. By then, I had already applied to train as a Sick

Children's Nurse (RSCN) at a children's hospital. I went to see the Allocation Officer who arranged placements. "For my medical placement," I started. "Um," she said cautiously. "Could I go on children's medical instead of adult? Because children's surgical is just children having operations, but medical is far more interesting and I've applied to do my RSCN straight after," I gasped out all in one breath. The allocation officer remained silent, looking at me whilst she deliberated my request. She moved across to a large chart on the wall whilst I held my breath. "Go on then," she said. I was delighted. It turned out that children's medical was short of students, so my request was convenient.

I bounced up the stairs to the children's ward on the first day of the placement. The staff welcomed me as they did not usually get third years. The junior sister was on duty that day, and asked me if I had ever done a baby bath. I had done thousands, but what should I say? Did they do them differently on this ward from maternity? I replied diplomatically and cautiously, "well, I have a bit of an idea, but I would prefer you to show me how you do them on this ward, so that I am doing them correctly." I was duly shown how to do a baby bath in the dinky little sinks in the baby bathroom. I was in trouble next day. The Sister rounded on me. "Why didn't you tell me you were a midwife and nursery nurse. Fancy letting me show you how to bath a baby". But what else could I have done on a first day? I wasn't going to brag or appear cocky. I never told ward sisters that I had previous training, so I don't know how she found out. I was really pleased when the Sister started calling me by my first name. It was quite unusual in those days to use first names for students, so I felt that I was really accepted. Anyway, she never could get her tongue round my surname, and always called me Swaley!

Oh, how I loved this ward. It was even better than children's surgical. The actual ward was not brilliant. It was an old Nightingale style ward in two halves, with offices, kitchens and stores in the middle. It was divided into the 'baby end' (under two's) and the 'big end' (older children). At the bottom of the ward was a playroom, which was used as a schoolroom and a dining room. The ward was on the first floor, there was no lift, and absolutely everything had to be humped up and down the stairs, which had an awkward bend in them halfway up.

The kitchen had a large window that overlooked the main drive into the hospital. Sitting at this window during a coffee or lunch break revealed what was going on in the hospital. The night staff found it even more riveting after a doctors' party. The nurses' home was opposite the doctors' home, so the night staff knew exactly who went where, and with whom. There is nothing like a hospital grapevine for spreading gossip! The further away from the truth it is, the quicker it spreads and is believed!

In the early fifties, the hospital had got its first children's doctor (Paediatrician). At first he did not have his own ward, but when he was given one, he asked for a lift, but was told that it would cost £500 and the hospital could not afford it. Besides, the building was condemned and it was only a temporary measure.

Very temporary. We moved in 1986, by which time the doctor had long since retired. He was a very easy going, pleasant, laid back man (most of the time), with a good sense of humour. Because he had been around a while, he was now seeing the next generation of children and recognised the parents as previous patients. Only small in stature, he made up for it in personality.

His secretary was a blind lady who was an absolute miracle woman. She was heavily involved with the local Brownies and Church, lived alone and worked full time. She even taught me to type, which is truly a miracle! By the late seventies, the first paediatrician was joined by a second one, who was the opposite of his colleague. Between them, they were an excellent combination.

One of the tests that I had to do on this ward was testing the urine of diabetic children. Nowadays, the test is usually blood rather than urine. The test at that time involved using a pipette and drawing five drops of urine, then adding ten drops of water into the test tube. Then you dropped a tablet into it, it fizzed up the tube, then settled down and changed colour - very pretty. The colour decided if there was any sugar in the urine or not. Whenever I did this test, I would depress the rubber end of the pipette and draw the water into the pipette, ready to count the ten drops.

You could bet your bottom dollar that you could get nine drops out of one pipette and then you would run out, so it was back into the water again. It was so frustrating. It happened everytime with me. I would hold my breath each time, but no, the water would stop. The exact number of drops is so crucial to the test that you could never leave it at nine. Collecting the urine was a work of art, too, especially if the child wasn't toilet trained. Sometimes it took you ages to collect some in a urine bag. This is a little bag that sticks on over the penis to collect urine on babies or toddlers. It's a lot harder in girls, a bit more hit and miss! Someone once asked me what my highest ambition was whilst I was counting the drops. I carried on counting. Seven, eight, nine. I don't believe it. Nine again. I savagely jammed the pipette back into the water before answering. "My highest ambition in nursing?" I asked, "why, to get ten drops of water into this pipette at one go." I am pleased to announce that I achieved my highest ambition, the very next day.

My three months were coming to an end all too quickly, and I was dreading going back to an adult ward. After my days off, the Sister asked to see me privately in the office. Oops, I thought, what have I done wrong. She was looking serious. "The Allocation officer rang whilst you were days off." My heart sank. Oh dear, where was she sending me? "The Allocation officer said that you were out of synch with the rest of the group, and all the wards were well staffed, so would you like to stay here for another three months. I have said 'yes' for you. I hope you don't mind, you can change it if you do mind", the Sister asked nervously. Mind, did I heck. It was all I could do not to kiss her! I thanked her profusely and breathed a sigh of relief. Oh the bliss of staying on my beloved ward for another three months. That would take me up to the exam, and I would never have to go on another adult ward again. I was ecstatic.

There were two Sisters on the ward, who were both very different. One was a young woman who was very intense, bubbly and rushed around. The other was slower, sedate, silver haired, with infinite patience. She had been on the ward for years and was well loved by patients and parents. She had a special affinity with adolescents, specially the troublesome ones. All the ward staff were a tremendous help to me as it got nearer to the exam. But I found I did not want to study adult nursing, but was devouring paediatric textbooks instead. Nine weeks before the exam, I decided it was instant cramming time. I made a detailed plan for revision. There was to be a three hour essay type question in the morning and a multi-choice question paper in the afternoon. I had already passed the mock exam or hospital finals as they were called, but needed some serious study.

The ward funds were at an all time low that spring and the hospital was having a sponsored slim. The Sister and I decided that as we were the plumpest members of staff, we would shed pounds to gain pounds for the ward. We were weighed in officially, and started the diet, checking up on each other and comparing notes. The weight started to creep off, but not as fast as we would have liked. On the second Saturday of the diet, we were on the late shift. We were quite busy and had not had time to go to the canteen. The Sister asked me if I would like to share a cheese salad for supper.

The next day we were both violently ill, and off work with diarrhoea and vomiting. We both had shigella dysentery. The doctors tried to blame it on our careless hand washing techniques. But we reckon it was the cheese salad! I have never been so ill. My own doctor warned me that he might admit me if I was no better the next day, and I thought 'no way.' By the next day I would have welcomed going in hospital, but it was not offered. I really thought I was going to die. Mum came to visit me to see if there was anything she could do to help. She sorted the Public Health man out, tidied round and made a meal for Jim. On leaving, she left me a book to while away the hours. On the first page of the book, someone died of dysentery. Thank you Mum.

But I was not too bothered once I got over the first week. The weight was pouring off. It was also a heatwave and the state finals were in four weeks. I spent the time outdoors. I spent half an hour on my back sunbathing, then half an hour on my front studying. Best of all, I won the sponsored slim! (Although some people who had to pay me said that I had cheated.) I would not recommend it as a slimming method, however.

During those four weeks, a friend's husband was changing his job as a drug representative, and had to thoroughly learn the structure and function of the skin. He made me learn it with him, despite my vigorous complaints because the skin never came up on state finals. It was usually an introductory block type of test question. The day dawned for the exam, and as I turned the paper over, I spotted a question 'Describe the structure and function of the skin, 40%.' Oh boy, thank you, thank you. It was so unusual to be on at all, but to give 40% weighting to the marks was even more incredible. The other 60% was about multiple sclerosis - a sad condition, but one that I had nursed, understood and also revised. I worked my way through the two papers and then came the inevitable wait.

On July 29th, the letter came. I had passed, thank God, which is just as well because I was starting my RSCN on August 27th, so I would have to get my notice in quickly. Fortunately, I did not have any sickness time to make up. There was a job vacancy on the children's ward but I knew I needed my RSCN if I wanted to stay in children's nursing long term. I rang the Allocation officer to see where I should go for the period of notice. I was sent to a surgical ward, so I was quite happy.

On the second Sunday, I decided to make a fresh fruit salad for all the patients. I collected donations of fruit and spent a happy hour making the salad, which the patients ate for afternoon tea. It was amazing, the ward did not give any bowel tablets out for days. However, whilst I was preparing the salad, I peeled the apples and ate all the skin, plus quite a bit of fruit myself. So soon after dysentery, it was too much for my delicate bowels. So off sick again I went, to complete my notice.

During this sickness, our family suffered another tragedy. Cynthia's husband of thirteen years, Edwin, had a heart attack and died at thirty-seven years old. Their daughters Lindsay and

Elaine were just six and four. The family closed together to help Cynthia during this awful time. It was with sadness and a sore heart that I left my training hospital to undergo further training.

CHAPTER FIVE

<u>CHILDREN'S HOSPITAL, HERE I COME</u>

It felt very strange to be leaving my training hospital and going to a different hospital, but I was looking forward to it all the same. By now, I was a whiz kid on the motor bike, but Mum was worried about me travelling as far as Manchester every day. She kept going on about buying a car, but I kept saying I could not afford it. My close friend Marian decided to sell her car, and she was in a financial position at that time to let me have the car then, and pay for it in instalments. (She has never been in that position since!) It was a very generous gesture, and made becoming a car owner a feasible option rather than a pipe dream. Marian's car had been her first ever car and was her pride and joy. It was a Mini 1275 GT and had been a rally car, so had twin petrol tanks that came in very handy during the petrol strike of 1979. It was also handy when buying petrol, because it didn't matter which side of the car was nearest to the pump, there was a tank on that side.

It was a royal blue car, with a white roof and gold 'go-faster' trim on the sides. The registration was KTB 111K, so Marian called the car Katie, or Katie B, or even Katie B. Good if she was misbehaving. On June 12th 1978, I became the proud owner of Katie, and decided to keep the name. Why do women have names for their cars? It is not a thing that men seem to do. Is this because men and women see cars differently, or is it that women tend to pick names for children and pets more than men? I have no idea. Answers on a postcard, please. But Katie she was. Marian grew to love the name so much that she called the baby she was expecting Katie, and she became my Goddaughter. Good job it was not a boy, and a good job she had not called the car Excalibur, or poor Katie would have been a laughing stock all her life. So there I was. The proud owner of my first set of wheels, and expensive it was too, to insure. Because it had a souped-up engine, the insurance was higher and I could only afford to have third party insurance, which was the biggest mistake of my driving career.

I duly set off to the children's hospital. It was a very easy journey from home if going on an early or late shift. However trying to get there for a 9 am start in School was a nightmare. I often set off at 7.15 am to get there, otherwise I was late for 9.00 am. As the journey is only 25 miles, on a good day, it could be done in 30-35 minutes but by 7.45 am the M66 was busy. I once sat through ten cycles of the traffic lights waiting to turn right through a busy junction. Only one car ever got through. It was many years before they added a filter.

I got to the hospital on the first morning, and found my way to the School of Nursing. The children's hospital is a double storey building, arranged around a very long corridor, with additional buildings in the grounds. The School was upstairs, around the middle of the long corridor. It consisted of three small classrooms, offices and a library. There was another general School of Nursing down the road which was much larger.

On the first morning, I asked to see the tutor. I explained quietly that I had been bereaved the week previously. If I appeared upset, quiet or distant, they were not to worry about me. I went into the classroom and found four rows of desks. There were ten students altogether and we all gravitated to the back of the class, as students do. Eventually the teacher came in, complained about our seating arrangements and told us to move to the front. Nobody moved. "Come on," she urged. So two of us moved to the front. The ten of us gelled instantly, and we were a very together group. By the second day, we were laughing so much that the tutor came in and told us off for making too much noise. She then gave me a very dirty look, and I felt guilty about having fun when I had had such a bad week before the course, but some of it was relief. When you are trying to support a thirty-one year old grieving widow who is very angry, it is not easy on the nerves. Sometimes it does you good to get right away from the situation.

The layout of the course was very similar to other training courses. Alternate theory blocks then placements. My first ward was to be a medical ward, which was a very similar ward to the one at my last hospital, so at least I would know what I was doing. Also, another of the wards was closed for repairs, and so two wards were being housed together. Thus I got the benefit of two different Consultants with different specialities.

I went on duty on my first day, quite nervous at being in a strange place. I went into the Sisters office and said hello to the night staff. A staff nurse with a very posh accent looked up at me. I asked where to put my bag, and an elegant manicured finger pointed to a cupboard. "Over there," she said in a very posh accent. Oh well, I thought, she looks miserable, but I suppose I do when I have just finished a night shift. Fortunately, the rest of the staff came in at that point.

The uniforms here were pale blue, which in most hospitals was the colour for staff nurses. Your rank was denoted by the number of red stripes on your hat. As post-registration (post-reg) students we wore three stripes like the third year students. Our badges showed that we were already qualified nurses undergoing further training. At the children's hospital, they wore disposable caps, so it was not the nail and finger wrecking activity that it had been previously.

When the late shift staff came on at lunch time, the Senior Sister sought me out. "Where's this nurse from my old training school then?" she asked and then promptly took me off to her office for a gossip. She had trained where I had and her parents still lived locally, so she wanted to know if people were still around, and whom we knew in common. I was there quite a while, and was getting dirty looks from the other staff. They probably thought I was lazy, but what can you do when you have been summoned by the boss? The sister told me that there was a staff nurse on the ward who also lived in my area, but she was on nights, so I looked forward to meeting her.

I settled down quickly into the routine of the ward. There was no necessity to have any experience with children prior to the course. My last six months of training on the children's medical ward stood me in good stead compared with some of my colleagues, who had little or no experience. The wards were old-fashioned, the children's hospital having been built at the turn of the century. The wards consisted of single cubicles, and larger bays that held several patients. Babies were usually nursed in a cubicle so that they did not pick up any infection from the other children. Babies' immune systems are immature at first, and what may be an ordinary infection to an adult or large child may overwhelm a small infant.

On my third week, I was travelling to work for an early shift, on a day of torrential rain, with great pools of water on the motorway. Suddenly, I found the car was out of control and I was aquaplaning. For those uninitiated, that means you have been driving too fast on water, and have actually taken off from the road. It was scary. The car started veering across the motorway from inside to outside lane, and nothing I could do would control it. Eventually I hit the middle barrier on the motorway, the car bounced backwards into the middle lane and stalled. I got out of the car, the radio still blaring, and stood in the middle lane. I stared at my squashed car and said, "this is the last straw, this is the last straw."

A voice shouted from the hard shoulder. "If you don't get off this motorway now, it will be the last straw." I came out of my reverie and looked about me. The traffic was still coming towards me and managing to swerve. I dodged on to the hard shoulder to my rescuer. She was a smart young lady with a brand new car. When she saw what was happening, she had pulled onto the hard shoulder to help. She was probably worried that I would hit her new car! I cannot remember now whether I thanked her or not, but I certainly thank her now, and have done many times since. She helped me get my car off the motorway. It was still driveable, so I got in and drove to work. I was worried that I was going to be late for work, when I was such a new student.

When I got to work, I hurried down to the ward, just in time for the handover from night staff. Sister could see I was agitated and when I told her why I was late, I burst into tears. I was immediately given coffee and sympathy and the miserable staff nurse on nights, Liz, offered to take me home again. "Oh, no thanks," I stammered, "I live a long way away." "I know you do," she replied, "I live near you, too." Trust me, I thought, waiting to find the local nurse, only to find it was the miserable one. My first impressions were exceedingly erroneous and we have remained close friends. (I am honorary aunt to one daughter and Godmother to the other). On that day Liz drove in front of me all the way to my garage to make sure I was okay. No mean feat when you have just done a night shift. What a friend. Because of her accent, Jim always calls her the 'Posh Piece,' a name that she was given by neighbours when she moved into a small village.

Pete, the garage mechanic looked at the car sadly. It was then that I remembered that I had not even paid a single payment on this car, and only had third party insurance. I told him that I needed the car mending very quickly and very cheaply. Pete said that if I was not too bothered about the colour, he could get me two wings from the scrap yard. He could get it back on the road within forty-eight hours and worry about a re-spray later. And he did have it back on the road two days later. I was delighted as I could not get to the children's hospital on the early shift by public transport.

This was the beginning of my donating a large part of my salary to Pete, as I had disaster after disaster with cars. Eventually Pete's Dad was made redundant and helped him in the garage. One day when I arrived, he shouted, "Oh look, the wage is here." I did feel as if I was paying their wages at times. I had been recommended to Pete by a doctor whose husband was a close friend of Pete's and he had only just opened up for business. He was married to Hilary, who was a nursery nurse that I had worked with years before. We nearly ended up related. The advantage of going to a one man garage is that you know he has done the work and not a young unsupervised apprentice, which could happen in the larger garages. The disadvantage of Pete's garage was that it was ten miles from home. I always had the complications of getting to and from the garage or killing time in town if it was a short repair.

The next time I broke down after the repair, I rang the RAC, explained my problem, and then they asked me for a description of my car. "Well," I replied, "It's royal blue, with a white roof, with gold stripes and one orange wing and one brown wing." There was a stunned silence at the other end of the line, then the operator said, "Well, at least we will have no trouble identifying you, Madam." As I became a regular caller to the RAC, I eventually got on first name terms with the local man. One day, he came out twice to me, and suggested I bought a new car, and changed to a garage nearer to my house! I eventually did both.

My first placement came to an end, and although I had learnt some things, it was very similar to where I had come from. I was going to the neuro-surgical ward next, and this was totally new. There were some very tragic cases on this ward including children with hydrocephalus (water on the brain). Babies with this condition usually have a shunt inserted from the brain, into the heart or intestines to drain off the excess fluid. This keeps the head to a normal size, but sometimes surgery is not suitable. It can be so difficult to hold or feed these children as their heads are so heavy.

Other children had been in car crashes or other road traffic accidents. Nursing these children could be very difficult because the parents often blamed themselves. It was necessary to spend a lot of time reassuring the families. Often the children had to be 'specialled', this was one-to-one nursing. Sitting by an unconscious patient, the time drags heavily for Mum and nurse. Most children made a full recovery, some were not so fortunate.

Some of the patients were admitted with spina bifida. This is where there is an opening on the baby's back or neck, and the spinal cord protrudes. It can be in varying degrees of severity, from having virtually no effect, to the patient being completely wheelchair bound, paralysed from the waist down. It is often linked to hydrocephalus. The children came in for closure of the wounds and for other reparative surgery.

Whilst I was on this ward, I was approached by another hospital nearby that specialised in cancer. They had a patient who lived in my area who was on a five day ward, and she was allowed home for the weekend. The mum had no-one who could help her with transport, so the hospital Social Worker approached me to see if I would take them home on Fridays. I then brought them back on Mondays, and I got PAID for my trouble. So it was mutually convenient as I did not get any travelling expenses normally. We all got very friendly, and it also gave me the opportunity for my highest pinnacle of driving expertise. The little girl was on water tablets and was always wanting to wee, usually urgently. One Friday night, I was driving past Kendal's department store, in the centre of Manchester, in the middle of the rush hour traffic. The little girl said that she wanted to wee. We only had a cardboard bedpan liner, but she sat on it, and filled it to the top. All throughout, I had to keep stopping and starting, to keep up with the traffic. And I never spilt a drop of wee! What a star! But have I received an honorary award from the advanced motorist's organisation? No, I have not!

At Christmas, I was put on night duty. The ward was very quiet, as all routine waiting list surgery was postponed until the New Year. There was a little boy in the ward aged about seven years, who virtually lived on the ward. He had had a lot of operations, and hardly got home between the operations. His home circumstances were poor as well, so life was difficult for him. He was a loveable, friendly little boy, who had learnt to make friends easily due to the constant stream of patients coming and going. I was on duty on Christmas Eve, and all evening he was laboriously writing a letter, tongue poked out between teeth, to Father Christmas. He showed me the letter, and I promised him faithfully that I would make sure Father Christmas got it. Eventually he settled off to sleep, and I removed the letter and composed an answer from Father Christmas. Oh the look of wonderment on his bright shiny face next morning, when he saw his letter. He made me read it out to him, then to all the other patients several times. I felt such a fraud, but at least it made his Christmas.

It was soon time to move on again. Back into School for another theory block. We were still a noisy group and tutors always commented that we were the noisiest group they had ever had. We decided to play on that and decided to do a sponsored silence. We knew we would get generous sponsors because nobody would believe that we could keep quiet for five minutes, let alone an hour. 'D' and I knew we were the worst offenders, so we put sellotape across our lips for the hour, whilst we sat in the dining room, posters aloft. When planning it, we needed a good cause to dedicate the money to. That day, we had listened to lectures on Cystic Fibrosis (CF), which is the commonest inherited childhood disease in England. These children produce too much mucous which clogs up their lungs and affects their digestion and pancreas. In years gone by children never survived to adult life, but with modern treatment, the picture is totally different and far more positive. In the nineties, the affected gene has been identified on the chromosome, so there is great hope for the future.

We contacted the local branch of the Cystic Fibrosis Research Trust to tell them of our plans, and they invited us to a meeting. We made over £100 and 'D' and I went to the next meeting to present the cheque. The Chairman of the group was one of the hospital doctors. He thanked us, saying that nurses do enough for caring for children with Cystic Fibrosis, without raising money as well, so they were doubly grateful. We were both very moved and started attending the group regularly. Whilst this was going on, a lady wrote to our local paper saying that her two year old son had Cystic Fibrosis and she would like to start up a support group. I contacted her and took her along to the children's hospital group for some years, before she started up a local group. Ironically, or thankfully, my local area has very few Cystic Fibrosis sufferers. For the number of children, there should be about forty to fifty cases, but there are less than ten, and most of them have moved into the area from other parts of the country.

The chairman became a valuable friend, who was always grateful for our support at the parents group, and lent or gave us books and invited us to conferences. Once, I asked him to check some writing I had done about Cystic Fibrosis. I had been at my friend Sheila's in the morning. Sheila's husband, Paul, was a drug representative who had a lot of dealing with the doctor as well. I took Sheila and Paul's middle boy Gregory along with me. As we were chatting, the doctor, a life long smoker, lit a cigarette. Gregory jumped into action and shouted "Mr Nicoteen says NO. No to smoking. Smoking Kills." It was so embarrassing. There was the middle-aged doctor quietly justifying his right to smoke to a toddler!

After the theory block, it was back to the wards. This time to the Burns Unit. I was a little worried about going there, in case there were some horrific sights. I need not have worried. The eight weeks I was there were the quietest they had ever had in the history of the unit. We spent a lot of time decorating the walls as I remember. And if I ever hear the theme from 'Bright Eyes,' I am transported back to the Burns Unit, because it seemed to be on the radio all day. I spent a lot of time with one boy - holding him, giving him cuddles and reading to him. He would cuddle in to you, and really relax. The unit had a toy tank, and when you wound it up, it played a cavalry charge, then made a lot of bangs and gun noises. It was brilliant. He and I loved it. But nobody else did. Mysteriously, everytime I went for coffee, it was moved out of the room, but I soon found it and put it back, much to his delight.

Some of the cases that were on the unit were very sad. It made nursing these children harder because the parents often felt guilty about the accident. They blamed themselves for not paying enough attention, or leaving the children to play unsupervised, or having matches in the house. Very often nothing could have prevented the accident, but the parents were still racked with guilt, especially where there was going to be scarring.

Whilst I was on the unit in May, it snowed heavily at home. Yes, in May. The M65 didn't exist then, and the M66 petered out at Rawtenstall, so to get to the motorway you had to get up a very steep hill, and go 'over the tops' on high land to Rawtenstall. This particular day, I tried all routes to get to work. The road to Accrington was blocked, the road to Todmorden was clear, but past Todmorden was blocked, so I gave up and stayed at my friend Marian's for the day in Todmorden. I'd rung work and explained that I couldn't get through. The next day, the roads were much better and I managed to get up the steep hill and over to the motorway. When I got to work, there was virtually no snow to be seen. It is a good job that they believed me.

My car, Katie, was beginning to go downhill rapidly by now. Before I got her, she was the family's second car, used to tootling about to the shops and schools. After a year of clogging up and down the motorway, she was showing signs of wear and tear. I put 18,000 miles on the clock in one year. She was using oil like there was no tomorrow, and Pete warned that it could be a sign of impending big and expensive trouble. Cynthia had bought a car from my step-father Joe, but was now buying a new one, so she let me have her car, on the same terms as Marian did. But this car didn't last much longer, and the 'big end' went on the motorway one night. It was going to be very expensive to mend, and I needed another car right away. Marian's husband John, was a car salesman, and he managed to get me an old clapped out, rust bucket of an orange Datsun. It saved my life. Without a car, I couldn't get to work. I was leaving home at six to get the first express bus at 6.20 am, but that didn't connect with the bus in the city centre to get me to the children's hospital in time for an early shift. So I got off at Rawtenstall, my stepfather picked me up and took me to work, then he went home and had his breakfast before going to Bolton to work at 9 am. I got myself home on the bus on the early shift, and to work on the late shift, but Joe picked me up after a late shift.

This carried on for ten days, until John saved me. The car cost £150, and didn't bring any guarantee with it, but it got me to work. John delivered it to the children's hospital for me, and then I realised my problem. I'd come on the bus in flip-flop slippers. As soon as I lifted the clutch, the flip-flop bent double and broke. So I had to drive home barefoot. I find it much better driving barefoot. Apparently, it saves petrol, because your foot is more sensitive to the pedal than your sole. Only trouble is, you get mucky feet! Well, you do in my mucky car.

In the summer, I spent eight weeks on the general surgical ward. I enjoyed the ward and did a short spell on nights during this time. One thing I didn't like about this ward was that you had to give the handover of your patients to the next shift without looking at your nursing notes. This wasn't so bad on days, because the children were up and about, and you got to know them, helping them with their treatments, and seeing their personalities. On nights, they were asleep for most of the time, so it was very, very difficult, as I have never been blessed with a good memory. The ward also confirmed to me again that I preferred medicine to surgery.

One little boy on this ward was a cutie. He was six months old. He had just had an operation and was not allowed any food or drink by mouth. All of his fluids were going into him through an intravenous line (a drip). One day, the consultant surgeon came to see him. She was a tall, elegant lady, with a dry sense of humour. When we went into the cubicle on the wardround, the little boy had disconnected the drip, and was sucking the end of the tube quite vigorously like a dummy. The consultant laughed and said, "I know I told you to give fluids through the drip, but I did mean the fluids to go into his vein, not his mouth." We were all very embarrassed by what had happened, but he suffered no ill-effects, so we all joined in the laughter, after we had sorted him out.

During the next theory block, we had a mock exam ready for the finals. On the morning of the exam, the car broke down and I only just arrived in time for the start of the exam. I was agitated but started answering the exam paper. The next week, I was mortified to find out that I had failed the exam. I had known the topic, so assumed that I'd made a mess of it because of being upset. That made up my mind. I would stay overnight for the real exam. I couldn't afford to fail the state exam because of an unreliable car.

My next placement was to have been on the Neuro-Medical Ward. I couldn't wait for this allocation, as it would help me deal with many of the children that I had seen at my training hospital. Many of the children with delayed development, handicap and epilepsy were referred to this ward. However, when the allocation list came out, I'd been put on the ward next door. This was the ward that had been closed earlier, and joined up with my first ward, so I'd already done that speciality. I flew off to see the Allocation Officer. All she said was "Tough," I argued my case, explaining how important it was that I did the other ward but to no avail. (Oh, where was the Allocation Officer from my training hospital, you were such a nice helpful Allocation Officer. I bet you'd have let me swap). But this lady was different. It was her mistake but she wouldn't let me swap.

I was bitterly disappointed, as I'd looked forward to the neuro-medical ward right from the first week of training, when we got our training plan with placements. Even though she acknowledged that it was her mistake, she wouldn't change it. So I went reluctantly to the other side of the ward, back onto a general medical ward. I didn't particularly learn anything new on this ward, but often the other ward was busy or short-staffed and I always volunteered to go and help out, so I could gain some limited experience. I remember one young boy on that ward. He couldn't stand the light at all, and lay with his eyes shut most of the time. Mum said she was going out to buy him some sunglasses. I felt so sorry for him that I went out to the car and lent him mine.

On one ward I worked on, we had a very good nursery nurse, who was brilliant with the children. One day she made jam tarts with the toddlers. When they were cooked, she handed them round all the visitors on the ward - Consultant, Physiotherapist, Pharmacist etc. We also took one to the Catering Manager, as a thank you for letting us have the ingredients. I declined the offer. After all, I'd seen the grubby hands and snotty noses that had accompanied the making of the jam tarts. How glad I was that I declined. All the lucky participants of the jam tarts were off sick the next day. But the children never ailed a thing.

Another day, the children did get ill. One fear in a children's ward is gastro-enteritis. It can be a killer if not caught in time. Suddenly, all the babies started being sick and getting diarrhoea. I was immediately suspect, as I had been looking after all the babies for the last day or two. Then we realised that it wasn't every single baby, but just most of them. So I was exonerated. If it was careless hygiene, they would all have been ill. The Doctor then received a message to say that the medical student was off sick, with the same germ as the babies. We'd got our culprit. He had only been in to certain babies, and that explained our mini-epidemic.

It was getting near the end of the fourteen month course. Although the travelling was crippling me financially, and whether the car would start was a constant worry, I decided I'd like to stay at the children's hospital, to consolidate what I'd learnt. Liz (Posh-piece) and I had become firm friends by then, and she worked three set nights a week. Sunday, Monday and Tuesday. For this, she got the same pay as full time days. If I worked the same nights, we could travel together, so that would be cheaper and I wouldn't be constantly worried about the car. I made enquiries and was welcomed by the night sister. I explained the set nights I wanted, and asked for the Burns Unit. She agreed. Two weeks later, a staff nurse was appointed for the same nights, so I wasn't needed. So I tried to work on Neuro-Surgery. The same thing happened again exactly as before. They were just about to open a High Dependency Unit, so I tried for there. And guess what? It happened again. I could have worked any other nights, but not the same as Liz, so it would defeat the object. Whilst all this was going on, someone rang me to say that both staff nurses were leaving to do their midwifery training, and there was a job going on the medical ward I had been on near my home. Humph, I thought, blow the children's hospital, I'll go back near home. And so I did. I only lived 1¼ miles from the hospital, so if the car broke down, I could WALK!!!

CHAPTER SIX

BACK TO ROOTS

My first day back on the children's medical ward, but this time in a pale blue staff nurses' uniform. I arrived early and put my bag away safely, changed into my uniform, and fastened my hat on. The phone rang. An emergency admission was on its way. It needed an oxygen tent. Oh boy, I thought. This is reality. I'm the staff nurse now, and I need to do the right thing. Fortunately, the staff nurse who was leaving, arrived at that point and helped me to get organised. Oxygen tents were cumbersome things. They comprised of a plastic box like a large bread bin, which was fastened onto the cot or bed-head. Attached to it was plastic sheeting in the shape of a box tent almost. The sheeting was draped over the frame, and tucked under the mattress to stop the oxygen leaking. The oxygen was then piped into the tent, to help the child breathe more easily. The plastic bread bin part was often filled up with ice, to cool and moisten the oxygen, so that the child's mouth and eyes didn't get too dry. Once you had set the equipment up, you then put the child into the tent through the long zips at each side and then zipped it up. As soon as you closed the zips, the child became frightened and hysterical, wanting Mum. Once the oxygen got going, the plastic tended to get misted up, so the child couldn't see out, and Mum couldn't see in. Then Mum would get hysterical and try and open the zips to comfort the child and the concentration of oxygen plummeted. It was an absolute nightmare. Fortunately, they have long since been confined to the museums and more sophisticated equipment is used nowadays. But on that first morning back, I was thrown in at the deep end. A baptism of fire.

I was in the peculiar position of having completed my RSCN training, but not having taken the exam. The exam was on the second day of my new job, so after having the baptism of fire, I had to go home and revise. Because of the disaster of the mock exam, I had arranged to stay at Sheila's house prior to the exam. At that time Sheila was the liaison Health Visitor for the children's hospital, and lived just down the road. If my car broke down, she guaranteed that she would take me to work for the exam. Paul was away at the time (as usual) so we had a good girls' gossip, rather than revision. We were sitting the exam at another hospital, along with the general students. The morning paper was brilliant. We got all the questions that we'd prayed for, especially one on burns. The general students were not so happy. They received an awful paper, and they were all miserable, being convinced that they had failed. They were all gutted. In the afternoon multi-choice paper however, our fortunes reversed. Their paper was straightforward and very generalised and ours was a stinker. The first ten questions were about very specialised care of a child with underwater seal drainage. None of us had ever nursed it, so we were all convinced we'd failed by tea-time.

In the meantime, it was back to the ward, with an eight week wait for the results. I settled back into the routine very quickly, and enjoyed being a staff nurse again, after years as a student.

This time though, I did not get a spotty sisters' hat, because I was an ordinary staff nurse, not a staff midwife. Staff nurses' hats were white with a blue stripe. Eventually, the day for the results came along and I stayed at home until the postman came. I nervously tore open the envelope. I had passed. What a relief. It would have been so embarrassing to have failed, when I was working as a staff nurse. I quickly rang Cynthia to tell her the news. She was delighted at the news, and so I rang Mum. Mum too was delighted and chattered away about it all being worthwhile. Suddenly she stopped and said "Oh, I'd better stop. You'll be wanting to ring Cynthia." "Oh, I've already rung Cynthia," I replied. There was a stunned silence at the other end of the phone. "You mean you've rung your sister before your mother?" asked my Mum, aghast. Oops. How do I get out of this one? To be honest, I was stunned. I never thought Mum was jealous like that. I started murmuring about Cynthia knowing what it feels like to get nursing exam results, and that is why I had rung her first. By then, Mum realised that she had sounded petty and backtracked. In the future I always made sure that Cynthia never told Mum I had rung her first, just to keep Mum happy. (I still rang Cynthia first, though, sorry, Mum).

My step-father, Joe, was far more practical. I owed money right, left and centre for cars, car repairs, tyres, etc. and he asked if I had the £75 needed for registration. I replied in the negative. Very generously he agreed to pay for my registration. I don't know why, but I was Joe's blue-eyed girl, and had become a Daddy's girl again. I don't know why it was me and not Cynthia, but I became the daughter he had never had, and always wanted.

Perhaps it was because I was available to go out with Mum and Joe more than Cynthia, who was always busy with babies and children. Mind you, he called me his <u>dearest</u> daughter. Not because I was more special than the others, but because I cost him more money! I cannot argue with that, but I always signed his cards as 'dearest daughter' after that.

When Cynthia had been widowed, she had just started going to church, and a forty year old bachelor, Peter, from the church helped wind Edwin's business up. Pouring over tax forms led to romance, and they married shortly after I returned to my local hospital. Cynthia thought Peter's Mum, Sally, might resent her. But she was delighted, and insisted on buying herself a little cottage near her friends. She adopted Lindsay and Elaine immediately and was ecstatic when first Richard and then Gillian came along - the grandchildren she thought she would never have. Sadly she died on Christmas Day, just after Gillian was born, so never lived to see them grow up.

On the ward, there was another 'new girl on the block' who was the wards Physiotherapist. She was a lovely, warm, gentle young lady and we were instant friends. Because we were both new, it helped cement the friendship. She was engaged to be married, and we all went to the wedding. Being very clever, she had her first baby Victoria on their 4th wedding anniversary, so when it is their Silver Wedding, it will be Victoria's 21st. Mind you, it did nothing for their wedding anniversaries, though, they were too knackered after Victoria's parties. These parties were often joint affairs with their second child, Philip, who was born two years later, but not on the same day. But I am running ahead of myself (as usual).

Another new arrival was the ward aide. We were one of the last wards to have a ward aide as a previous sister had declined to have one. I don't know why, because ours was the best thing since sliced bread. She was calm, unflappable, pleasant, methodical and took away much of the time-wasting administration jobs. We used to dread her having any holidays as we had to revert to doing her job.

Six months after I had got back to the ward, one of the consultants decided to retire as a Paediatrician, as he was sixty-five. Not that he retired as a Doctor, because he was working as a Locum when I was having an operation in 1995 - he was eighty-one years young. He will never be old. Fortunately, he was only checking that I was fit for surgery and not actually doing the operation! He decided to retire on the 31st March, and on that day, the new Consultant came on the ward rounds to meet everyone. He came to work on his first day as Consultant on April 1st. He said a polite 'good morning' and sat in the doctor's office opposite the sister's office, twiddling his thumbs, not quite sure what he should be doing. "Would you like a coffee?" I asked innocently. "Oh yes," he replied gratefully, "that would be lovely." I hurried to the kitchen and got the specially prepared coffee, that looked lovely but was stone cold. Well, it was April 1st, and we had decided that we should start as we meant to go on.

Unfortunately, he has asbestos tonsils, and always downs a coffee in large gulps. As the cold coffee hit his throat, he sprayed it straight back, all over the office, whilst we all fell about laughing. We were laughing so much that we nearly forgot to say April Fool, before apologising. I then asked, "Shall I go and get you your real coffee now?" "Yes," he said suspiciously, "and what have you put in that one, Lasix?" (Lasix is medicine to make you wee a lot). "Oh no," I said, "there is nothing in it, but that's a good idea." He decided he did not trust me, and followed me into the kitchen to watch me make the coffee. At least it set the tone, and broke the ice. We laughed about it for days, and the children thought it was terrific. He specialised in chest disorders with a specific interest in asthma and cystic fibrosis. Whilst we did not have many children with cystic fibrosis, we had hundreds with asthma. (Don't know whether it was the genes or the weather). He took over their care, helped by the new physiotherapist, who was also an expert in these areas. They worked well together and eventually did some research on children's asthma locally and had a chapter published in a book about it.

The ward routine carried on. One of the Sisters had quite a lot of time off sick and on maternity leave. Out of those two years, she only actually worked ten months, so I was often the second senior person after the Sister. This meant that I got a lot of management experience. There were very few trained staff in those days, and we relied on large numbers of students to make up the numbers. The poor students really were thrown in at the deep end. The staff comprised of two staff nurses besides me, plus an enrolled nurse and an auxiliary. There was also a cleaner, a nursery nurse, and a schoolteacher. We were all very good friends and worked well together. There was none of the bitchiness that was present on many wards where a lot of women work together. There was no-one on a power trip, or moody, so life was easy and happy. As I had been working opposite the Sister for much of the time, I was working more or less as a junior sister, without getting the pay or benefits. When I heard that there was a sister's post going at another local hospital, I thought 'Why not'. I duly applied and was summoned for interview. On the morning my car would not start. Mega panic. What could I do? I rang Liz (Posh-piece) up and asked her if she could help me. Fortunately, she was not in bed. She ran me over to the interview and got me there just in time. I felt as if the weight on my shoulders that I had had at the children's hospital had returned. At the end of the interview I said that I wished to withdraw my application. I couldn't stand the worry about cars again.

Eventually, one Sister left to go into teaching. So a Sisters post was available in my own hospital. The other Sister encouraged me to apply. After a nerve-wracking interview, I was given the job. The other candidate had been working as a midwife so was temporarily out of paediatrics. I was absolutely delighted, but a little worried about the extra responsibility. I wore my new navy dress with white trim, and got back my spotty sister's hat. After being in white or pale blue all my nursing career, it felt very strange to be in navy. I hated walking into the canteen for the first time, feeling as though everybody was making comments.

But I soon became used to it, and you certainly get a lot more respect when you are a Sister.

We had a wide range of children from nought to sixteen years. Some were tiny vulnerable babies, others stroppy adolescents. I always preferred the baby and toddler end and the other Sister preferred the older children and adolescents, so we were a good team. In the late seventies and eighties, not as many Mums stayed overnight so getting through the early morning routine was often a nightmare. We tried to get them all bathed before 9 am and then we could leisurely feed them all after their baths.

Our ward was quite in advance of many hospitals in that we had a mother and baby cubicle built with en-suite facilities in the late seventies and we had relaxed the visiting hours so that parents could come and be with their children for as long as they wanted. Being in hospital can be a very frightening experience for small children, especially if they cannot understand why they are there. They only know that Mum has disappeared and strangers are doing hurtful things to them. Having a parent around makes a tremendous difference to the child's experience. Many children who were in hospital in the forties and fifties with no, or very little, parental contact during their admission, suffered the effects of anxiety and separation. Sometimes the effects could last through into adult life, resulting in a life-long fear of hospitals and doctors. Because it was recognised that separation was causing psychological damage, the rules were gradually relaxed to allow parents more contact with their children in hospital. But some hospitals were quicker than others to relax their rules.

We had a very wide range of conditions, with some very unusual ones that were extremely rare. These were often the inborn errors of metabolism that I had learnt about whilst I was a nursery nurse. Whilst I was at this hospital, I was very fortunate to be awarded a scholarship to go for further study. I chose to study inborn errors of metabolism at a children's hospital. It was a very valuable experience and not only inflamed my interest, but was also very useful in nursing the children that came into my own ward.

One small group of patients that we nursed were children with Thalassaemia. This was a grim disorder which was inherited and affected Greek Cypriots and Asians. The children had defective haemoglobin which caused their red blood cells to break down too rapidly. Thus the children were always anaemic and feeling run down. The treatment was to give the children blood transfusions, which they had to have every week or two. Their lives were quite miserable as they had to attend regularly for blood tests as well as the transfusions.

The problem with repeated blood transfusions was that they had their own iron stores, plus the iron in their diet, plus the iron from the donor blood. The body cannot cope with too much iron and stores it in muscles and joints. The children then got terrible side-effects from the iron overload with the result of an early death from heart failure, when the heart became affected. I saw a dramatic change in the treatment of this condition whilst I was working.

A treatment was introduced that got rid of the excess iron from the body. Initially, this was just given after a transfusion, but it didn't have much overall effect on the iron levels. It was decided to introduce daily treatment for these children which could be carried out at home. The results were quite dramatic as the dangerous iron levels fell. It was our job to teach the parents to give the treatments at home, to prevent them having to come into hospital as often. Eventually, bone marrow transplants became available for these children which had a terrific impact on their survival rate. We went from nearly always having a child in with Thalassaemia, to never seeing them again, as all our little 'regulars' had successful bone marrow transplants. From being a grim disorder where death was usually the outcome, in my own career, I saw a dramatic turnaround for these children which made nursing them so much easier.

The death of a child was always something we dreaded and fortunately it was not very common. It is the one aspect of children's nursing that puts people off considering it as a career. People will say to you, "I couldn't cope with children dying, you must be hard." Well, no, you are not hard, and it is never easy. Fortunately, it is not a major component of the job in a children's ward in a general hospital. In a regional cancer ward, it may be more common, even with today's terrific survival rates. There is no set way of learning to care for a dying child and its family. You only learn by dealing with it, although lessons on care of the dying can help and give you the theoretical background. By working with the families, you work through your own grief, whilst the family are working through theirs. Whilst you never become used to it, and certainly never get hard, you learn how to cope with it yourself, and the experience you gain, then helps other families. Learning is often by gut feeling. You try something and see if it helps that family. Sometimes you get it wrong. It's often a matter of knowing your family and how they will react, but you do not always have that advantage, if the child has been admitted as an emergency. The child and family can teach you so much, making you feel very humble in the process. Sometimes it was a brand new patient who died unexpectedly or suddenly. That could be a very difficult situation because you were shocked as well. Often there was no time to get to know the parents and it was difficult to know how to deal with them, or how they would react. People often react differently during grief anyway, so even if you have known the patient and family very well, trying to care for them can be hard. You desperately want to help ease their burden and will try anything that you think will help them.

At other times, it was a patient who had been a constant or regular visitor to the ward. Some patients stayed on the ward for months and almost became part of the family. Indeed, when one of these patients died it felt like you had lost a family member. Some families welcomed or even expected you to go to the funeral. For me, that always helped, as I felt that I was paying my last respect and showing caring concern for the families.

As some of our children stayed under the care of paediatricians until almost adulthood, it changed the way we dealt with the family when the young person was dying. Whilst the care of the parents might be the same, the older youngsters had very different needs when approaching death than a younger child. It was a humbling experience to watch these youngsters go through the grieving process about their own death. They would 'set their house in order', often giving their personal possessions away to their nearest and dearest. Some even planned their own funeral.

Our focus was on the parents and children primarily, but there were two other groups of people that had to be considered. Firstly, the siblings. Whilst the dying child was ill, the sibling could have been passed from pillar to post, from relative to relative. Some families won't tell the siblings what is happening, but the children often know anyway. The sibling could start thinking that they have caused their brother or sister's illness and get guilt feelings.

The other group of people that needed special attention were the grandparents. They had the awful burden of the impending loss of a grandchild, which is about losing your future. Many grandparents would pray that the illness could be transferred to them, and they would be prepared to die, if only it would save the life of their grandchild, who had all their life still to live. But as if this wasn't enough, they have to watch their own child trying to come to terms with the death of their child and not knowing how to help them. A sort of double whammy of grief.

They want to help, but don't want to intrude. Thus, when caring for the dying child, the whole family had to be looked after. Sometimes it was not just family, but close friends as well.

But it was not all doom and gloom, and we had a lot of fun and laughs. Working with children is always so. The ward rounds were carried out nearly every day and often could get monotonous, but usually the children made them more lively. The worst of all were Monday morning ward rounds. They went on all morning. Woe betide you if you had not had your breakfast before 9 am, because you'd had it 'til lunchtime then. Eventually, a third paediatrician joined the team. It amused the first paediatrician that there were now three paediatricians, when he had worked single-handed for many years, but to be honest, the workload had increased tremendously in that time. On a Monday, all three paediatricians would go on a joint wardround together and see every patient together. That's why it took all morning!

It was good for the patients, because they were getting the benefit of a second and third opinion on their child, whereas on the adult wards, this never happened. It was also good for the doctors, because they knew all the children who were going through the wards, in case they were called out to them in an emergency. Sometimes an irate parent would demand a second opinion if they were disgruntled, but these children had already had more than that.

One day we had rather a lot of Asian babies in the ward. The Mums always lived in with their babies but often could not speak much English. On this particular day, an Asian gentleman followed us round on the ward round and helped us tremendously by translating for the Mums. Later I realised he was still on the wardround, when we were seeing all the other babies. He was just plain nosy and enjoying finding out what was going on! Another day we lost a paediatrician. It was his patient that we were seeing next but he was nowhere to be found. We eventually found him playing Connect Four with one of the other doctors patients. It was not even his own patient! When I think back to the adult wards, and the way some of the consultants expected to be treated like Gods (and still do!), I am just glad I chose paediatrics.

Every six months, the junior doctors changed. The doctors who came to paediatrics were either heading for a career in paediatrics or training to be General Practitioners. General Practitioners have to spend a further three years in hospital after qualifying, as Senior House Officers on a rotational scheme. They go to areas like paediatrics, medicine, surgery, casualty, psychiatry, skin disorders, so that they will have a lot broader base to their knowledge. The doctors used to rotate every six months on February 1st and August 1st. It was some years before I realised that the other Sister was usually on holiday for both those dates. I do not know whether it was intentional or not, but I remember groaning and thinking - here we go again.

The training of new doctors was a delicate task. Technically they were trained by the consultants, but we always reckoned that we nurses had a role in it too. Doctors varied tremendously. The ones we liked best were those who asked our advice. The ones we liked least were the ones who knew it all, would not listen to advice and thought they were God's gift to the medical profession. Some of them were absolutely petrified of being on the children's ward and some took to it like a duck to water. Each senior house officer (SHO) was based on a ward, and then there were registrars, as well as the consultants.

Whoever said that you shouldn't work with children or animals was probably a very wise person, as we had some funny experiences. One of the funniest episodes I witnessed was when a paediatrician came to examine the back of a baby's eyes. I held the baby's eyes open whilst the doctor looked into them.

Suddenly, there was a splashing noise and I could feel a spray on my arm. I looked round and realised that the baby was weeing right up into the air. The wee was falling in an arc on to the doctor's head and dripping off. I leaned over to the sink to get some wet paper towels. I was laughing hysterically by now and the doctor realised what was happening. "Oh God, oh God," he kept saying. "Oh don't be so soft, it's only a bit of wee, it won't harm you," I replied. "It's not the wee I'm bothered about" he said, "it's the fact that you've witnessed it, I'll never live this down. You'll tell everyone about it." Cut to the quick, I replied that I would not.

The next day on the big Monday ward round, the doctor <u>actually</u> <u>asked</u> me what the baby's stream of urine was like. (What a short memory). "Well actually," I replied, "I promised not to tell, but since you have specifically asked, this baby can wee right up into the air and on to your head." "Right, okay, that's enough, I remember now," interrupted the doctor. But too late, the tale was told at his own request and I had not broken faith!

Another funny episode that I witnessed was when I heard a loud screaming at the entrance to the ward. I rushed to see what was happening. I saw a child gripping the edge of the door-frame, whilst his mother tried to pull him off. When I asked what the matter was, she said that he didn't want to go home! Perhaps we have made children's wards too nice nowadays.

Often we would have laughs with the children at the funny things they said, or their interpretation of what was wrong with them. Very often we had to explain things to a child at a level which they could understand. How do you explain to a child that they need a drip or a blood test? Sometimes we would use play to explain things to them. I wish that I had £1 for every time I've put a drip up on a teddy, or given them a name-band, or a nebuliser. I could retire now. But if it happens to Teddy, it is often more acceptable to the child and they will let you do the procedure to them. If the child was too small to understand, it was very difficult to prepare them at all. It just meant that you had to give lots of extra cuddles afterwards, to help relieve the pain or fear.

One group of children that we often had in the ward were those with mental handicap or learning difficulties/disabilities or special needs as we now call them. Sometimes, the diagnosis completely rocked the family and they found it very difficult to cope. Family dynamics and relationships change as the child becomes the focus around which the whole family revolves. It often makes or breaks a relationship. Marriages and relationships often took the strain and a parent could be left on their own to cope. The majority of parents are absolutely marvellous. They never complain about their lot and cheerfully care for their children. Many parents of children with severe learning difficulties say that they receive extra strength to cope, and if they had known what was going to happen they would have thought that they could not cope. Caring for a child with learning difficulties or disabilities is a full-time job in itself, and I was always amazed how these families could still have a relatively normal life, despite their added responsibility. We had many regular children who attended the ward with learning difficulties. Usually they came in following a fit, or if they had an infection.

Sometimes the children would stay in hospital after a fit so that the doctors could stabilise the treatment for the fits. The doctors would try a new drug and it would work well. But after a few weeks, it would wear off - the so-called honeymoon period. Then it was back to trying a new drug, or more usually, a combination of drugs, to get the right formula for each child. No two children were ever the same. What worked for one child would not necessarily work for another. It was a very frustrating event for doctors and the parents, but even more so for the children.

One of the problems for children with learning difficulties is that they outgrow the paediatric wards. There aren't any doctors dealing with adult learning difficulties, and so the children tend to stay under the care of the paediatricians. One of the paediatricians was a specialist in children with delayed development, but once the children were large, it was difficult to know where to treat them. It was inappropriate to have them on the children's ward, but there was nowhere else for them to be nursed. It often happened that they still came to the ward in their twenties, although this does not happen now.

The same thing happened to children with Cystic Fibrosis (CF). By the early eighties', they were surviving into adult life. The adult doctors had not caught up with the knowledge necessary to care for children with CF who had survived. Nowadays, the children are transferred to the adult physicians when they leave school. As treatment has progressed, the children survive much longer. Whereas when I first started working with children with CF, they rarely survived their teens. Changes in treatment included giving antibiotics every day to keep the bugs at bay. Initially we used to bring the children in every three months for two weeks to have stronger antibiotics straight into the vein through a drip. This was very restrictive for the children, and caused a loss of schooling as well. It was mighty inconvenient for the parents, too. Eventually, as a home nursing team for children was set up, the parents and/or child were taught to give their own drugs at home. This has been a major improvement in the quality of care for these children, as they can get on with their lives between doses of drugs.

One thing that hasn't changed over the years is Christmas, and we had some good times. If you have to work as a nurse on Christmas Day, then the children's ward is the place to be. It's great fun. There was not a great deal of routine on any day, but there was none at all on Christmas Day. More or less, it was anything goes - within reason. Most of the families stayed all day and it was chaos. Obviously we tried to send the majority of children home and the doctors even did ward rounds on Christmas Day to see if any children could be discharged. Children admitted on Christmas Eve used to be very concerned that Father Christmas would not be able to find them, and we would have to give a lot of reassurance. Because the majority were sent home, those that were left were pretty sick.

One Christmas Eve, I spent nearly a whole evening trying to arrange transport for a mother whose child could not go home and mum had no transport to visit on Christmas Day. I even rang the Chief Nurse when every other avenue had failed. He wasn't fazed by my call and authorised a taxi for mum the next day.

Another Christmas, we had loads of poorly babies in and we just spent all day tube feeding one after another. In the end, we took the sickest babies into the kitchen with us, so that we could get something to eat ourselves. Another Christmas, the 'baby end' was full and the 'big end' empty. All the babies bar one were Asian and Moslem, so they were not celebrating Christmas. We decided to concentrate all our efforts on the remaining baby who was in the cubicle. He had been very ill and as he was an only child, both parents had stayed. We told them of our intentions to spoil them for the day, and they both looked embarrassed. They were Jehovah's Witnesses, and did not celebrate Christmas. It was a funny old Christmas that year, but the staff enjoyed themselves.

Father Christmas always visited the ward, but one year we got two together. We had some very confused children that year. Each year we had a party before Christmas, and invited all the regulars to come. It made a nice change for them to come when they did not need blood tests or treatments. Our regular Father Christmas at the parties was a porter. He was a very gentle man with the children and they all loved him. Sadly, he had to take early retirement when he developed a degenerative disorder. Did he sit at home, feeling sorry for himself and bemoaning his fate? He did not. He sits in his wheelchair in the out-patients' department every week as a 'welcomer'. He welcomes the patients with his big cheery smile as they arrive and helps those who are unsure of where to go or are anxious. What a star!

At one of the Christmas parties, we all got dressed up in fancy dress. I was Scarlett O'Hara. I looked very becoming in my bright red, off the shoulder crinoline, but unfortunately the ward was so busy that I never got into the actual party. Changing drip bags and squeezing my crinoline into a cubicle was quite trying, to say the least.

April Fools Day was always a dangerous time on the ward. The doctor that I had April Fooled usually tried to avoid coming until after 12 noon. Before a new paediatrician started, he got very twitchy and kept asking what tricks I was going to play on the new paediatrician when he started on the ward. We were bemused by his reaction until he reminded us that we had April Fooled him on his first day, (as if we would ever be allowed to forget). We reassured him that there would be no tricks - after all the new paediatrician was starting on May 1st, not April 1st. A much wiser man. Perhaps he had heard about us.

We were at risk not only from the children, but also the doctors. An SHO rang to say that a child with diabetes was coming in who was very sick. The Sister took the call and told me about it. I dashed off to the treatment room to get all the equipment ready, when the Sister stopped me. "Don't be fooled," she said, "that patient never comes in through the doctor or casualty, he always rings the ward for advice first." She was right, the patient never arrived, and a crest-fallen doctor arrived shortly after. That was one April Fool trick that I would have fallen for, but for the Sister's astute knowledge.

One day I got a phone call and I thought it was the registrar. The voice on the phone was very posh (just like the registrars) and said that he was ringing from the Ministry of Defence. I decided to play along, and in my plummiest voice I replied "Oh yes, how can I help you?" The voice then proceeded to ask me if we had had a new patient admitted, and gave me a name. If the child was present, could I give details of her condition. Oh no! It really was the Ministry of Defence. I followed the hospital procedure for checking on the enquiry before giving information. He explained that a soldier was due to go on a tour of duty the next day, but had rung up asking for sick leave to be with his child. He explained rather sheepishly that some soldiers would use an excuse like this to get out of a tour of duty. But this was genuine. When the officer heard that the child was genuinely sick he granted instant sick leave, and asked me to convey the information to the father. I encouraged him to ring back anytime for a progress report. The most amazing part about this episode is that I kept my mouth shut until I realised it was genuine. I am not known for my reticence or lack of something to say, but I am just glad I did not tell the man from the Ministry to shut up and stop mucking about.

Another year I thought I was the butt of an April Fool joke, which also turned out to be true. I got a phone call on March the 31st from the Lancashire Evening Telegraph. This was a local paper, and the journalist rang to say that I had been nominated to receive a Lancashire Evening Telegraph New Years Honours List award. He promptly interviewed me about my work, and why I thought I had been nominated. Highly embarrassed, I said that I had not got a clue, and that I only did a job of work. He talked a while and than said that he would be in touch in the near future. I thanked him and then rang off.

I was feeling really pleased that somebody had taken the effort to sponsor me when I noticed the date on the calendar. "O.K." I thought, "March the 31st, this will be an April Fools joke, which one of them has done this?" But it turned out to be true. I, and about twenty other locals were taken out for a meal, with our guests, and all presented with an inscribed goblet. It was a very proud moment, especially for Mum who came with me. Mum was in her element, basking in reflected glory. Oh, can't Mums be embarrassing? But all the relatives were the same, and do you know, all the recipients were like me. They could not believe why they were there, because they thought that they had done nothing out of the ordinary. Indeed, a lot of them seemed to be doing far more than me, such as a handicapped lady who did a lot of voluntary work. The most embarrassing part of it was that they did a small article about me in the local paper headed 'Linda's a Perfect Angel'. The children on the ward found out about this and made me a pair of wings, a halo and a big badge saying 'Perfect Angel'. I was made to wear them all day long. At least it cheered the ward round up, but I drew the line when they suggested that I wear them to go to the canteen..

When I first started nursing, nurses were not allowed to accept money for the ward as it was seen as unprofessional, neither were they allowed to fund-raise. But as resources became limited and equipment costs soared, there was a change of heart. Suddenly it was O.K. to go to the pub to collect a cheque for the ward, or assist in fund-raising yourself outside the hospital. Through funds that were donated to the ward I set up a nebuliser bank. A nebuliser is a little chamber attached to a machine that gives drugs in minute particles, so that the drug can get to parts that other drugs cannot reach - a bit like Heineken! It was used for children with asthma, and revolutionised the care that we gave to the children. Preventative drugs like Intal could be given through the nebuliser to keep the children healthy and out of hospital. Other drugs to help a child during an asthmatic attack could also be given, thus preventing a severe attack and preventing hospitalisation.

I was so impressed by this new treatment that I was inspired to write an article for the nursing journal - Nursing Mirror. I was totally amazed when it was accepted, and even more pleased when I got a fee. It was such a buzz to see my name in print for the first time. I kept going into the newsagents to have another peek. Because of this, a local paper interviewed me and wrote a piece about my nebuliser bank. Although we were prescribing the treatment for the children, they were not provided on the NHS. - a fact that we thought was deplorable, but one that we could not alter. So it was off on the fund-raising tours, to buy nebulisers to loan to the families. At one stage my Aunty Helen rang and asked me if I was having an affair with the newspaper photographer because my picture was in each edition!

When we went to collect a cheque, we were not 'trusted' and had to be accompanied by a hospital administrator. We went to many functions together. At one function, the administrator mentioned that there had been a comment by a colleague that he was always in the local paper. I argued that I was in as much, if not more than him. He threw down the gauntlet. For the next month, we would keep a check on how many times we had been in the local press, and compare notes at the end of the month. We did not decide on a 'prize' but both decided to think about a suitable one.

Throughout the time I had been back from the children's hospital, I had been going to night school for something or other each year to keep my brain active. Sometimes it was just an 'O' level, but I began to wonder about a career in nurse teaching. If nurses obtained a diploma in nursing and a teaching certificate, they could automatically register as a clinical teacher. I thought that this would be a lovely job, as I really loved the teaching side of my role, but did not want to lose my clinical skills. I never felt that I did enough teaching on the ward due to the time factor. I applied for the first year of the two year diploma course. It entailed attendance at the local college of further education on one day a week. There were three subjects. The history of nursing, psychology, and physiology (how the body works). They were all subjects that involved a lot of studying, especially the physiology. A large proportion of students failed the physiology and I was no exception.

The biology teacher, was brilliant and gave me individual coaching for the re-sit. Most of the candidates that passed scraped through on a 'C'. The first time I got an 'E'. (My friend Tilly got a 'B' first time, but then that was typical of Tilly, clever beggar). When I re-sat the exam, I was pretty convinced that I would have failed again. In the September I enrolled for the teaching course, which was also held at the local college, and taught by our psychology teacher. The second week of the course, the physiology results came out and I had got a 'B'. I could not believe it and kept walking round the house saying "a 'B', a 'B'."

Unfortunately, by this time I found out that the diploma course was changing, and the old diploma was being phased out. The second year of the diploma course was not run locally, only at nearby towns. I rang both colleges, but they had already stopped doing the course. Trust me, always in the wrong place at the wrong time. The only place that was still running the course was Huddersfield. I rang the course tutor and was told that the final course had started three weeks before, but I was welcome to join. Indeed, if I joined it would ensure that the course carried on as there was the bare minimum number of students on the course. I knew that now I had signed up for the teaching course I would not be allowed to swap, as it would prevent someone else doing the teaching course, and waste the fees. The hospital were very good at paying for nurses' further education and personal development, but were not too keen if you did not complete, understandably.

Thus started one of the hardest years of my life. I worked four days on the ward, spent one day at college locally and one day at college in Huddersfield, and had one day off a week. The ward staff were very good about the off-duty, ensuring that I was able to get to class most weeks. They were both gruelling courses, with a lot of work attached to them. As well as the course work for the teaching certificate, we had to log up thirty hours of teaching, some supervised by our teacher and some by other experienced teachers. I was fortunate because the nursery nurse course ran in the same college, and I was able to carry out my teaching easily. Some of the students found getting groups to teach very difficult. The class comprised of two-thirds nurses and one-third other people. We had a man with a doctorate in computing, a beauty therapist, two flower arrangers, a musician, and graduates wanting to get back into work after bringing up their children. I usually sat with Marge and Maureen. Little did we know at that time that the three of us would all work together as teachers of nursing, but that was a long way in the future.

The tutor at Huddersfield, Mike, was great. He was so laid back he was horizontal, but he taught us all so much. He really stretched us all mentally, and made us think for ourselves, and wider and deeper than previously. I was approached by the nursing press about this time to write a piece about what had helped me during my nursing career, and Mike was one of the people that I mentioned in the article. We were taught a whole new way of looking at nursing. Strangely, there was a parallel mix of students in that group. We were like Noah's Ark. Two of everything. Two medical nurses, two surgical nurses, two mental health nurses, two health visitors and two paediatric nurses. Thus when there was any group work to be done, he was able to split us up into our specialities, to discuss the issue. It also meant that we had a very broad knowledge of the other specialities.

For this exam, you had to produce two case-studies about patients who you had nursed. Then you had to do a written exam about the effects of disease on health, and also an exam on your speciality. As if that was not enough, you then had to go to London for a fifteen minute oral, to discuss your case-studies. Yes, all the way to London. Not as easy as slipping over the Pennines. Lynn, the other paediatric nurse and I decided that we would travel down on the morning of the oral. However, when our appointments came, they were for 11 am and 11.30 am, so we were a little worried about getting there on time. My Manchester friend, Sheila, had by now moved to Bury St. Edmunds. Her husband, Paul, had been promoted and moved down to head office. So we stayed there overnight, and drove to the first underground station the next morning. Leaving the car at the station, we took the tube into the city, to get to the exam. The first thing we saw in London was that there had been a one day lightning strike by British Rail, and all inter-city trains had been cancelled. Thank God that we had stayed at Sheila's, as there was a rule that if you did not turn up for the oral, you failed the whole course, and no excuses were accepted! It's funny how Sheila always seemed to get me to the exam on time.

The oral was nerve-wracking but nowhere near as bad as the midwifery one. It was carried out by nurses, with not a consultant in sight. Nevertheless it was gruelling, and once again, you could not tell how you were doing. At long last the results were out for both courses and I had passed them both. Mike, the tutor rang to say that my article giving him a mention arrived by the same post as the pass list for the Diploma. It was

100% success rate, so the two things made him a very happy man. I was totally and utterly exhausted after a year with only one day off each week, and two lots of course work, and teaching, and preparation, and work as well. I vowed that I would never do any courses ever again. It was then that I found out that the automatic qualification of clinical teacher from the diploma and teaching certificate had stopped in May. I had missed it by weeks. But then that's the story of my life, isn't it? Couldn't even get born on time!

CHAPTER SEVEN

<u>HERE WE GO AGAIN</u>

During the summer I had felt a feeling of freedom. No studying, no deadlines, no essays, no lesson preps. For once I had time for myself - to read novels and knit to my heart's content without feeling guilty. Tilly rang to tell me about a course that she had seen advertised. It was a research course at Manchester University, especially for nurses. Tilly tried to persuade me to go. 'No chance' I said, "besides, I don't want to do any research." Tilly explained about the course and said that even if I did not want to do research myself, I should learn about it for its own sake. "Well anyway," she said, "I am going whether you go or not." I cannot remember now at what point I weakened, but come September, I was off to University with Tilly every Monday night.

Mondays were not a good day to go to nightschool. I rarely got off early, and for many years, I had done the late shift on a Monday. The first night we learnt about the format of the course, and the importance of research to every practising nurse. The second week was spent in the massive library. We had a lecture on the layout of the library and how to use it. At the end of the lecture we were told that because we were part-time students, we could not borrow any books! What a waste of three hours! But we were allowed to <u>look</u> at the books and use them in the confines of the library. Big deal.

The fifth week of the course was Bonfire night. During the day we had been talking about a colleague's wedding and I was jealous because she was having nearly a month off work. We also talked about the ward night out, and bemoaned the fact that long dresses were out of fashion, as they felt much more dressy and feminine. I was to remember that conversation later. Tilly and I set off for Manchester, late as usual because we had both been working. In honour of the day, I had made a tin of bonfire toffee to take to nightschool with us, and it was on my knee. It was Tilly's turn to drive, and we chatted as we went along. We were talking about our long-term career plans. I said that eventually I would like to do a degree, but I could not stand the thought of studying part-time after I had done a day's work. Tilly asked how I would get funding, and I told her that I had approached my step-father, but he would not support my cause. We were approaching a set of traffic lights and the lights were changing to amber as we drove through.

*　　*　　*　　*　　*　　*

Suddenly I woke up. I looked round the strange room. It was a high ceilinged room, with white tiles on the walls. There was a small window at the top of one wall opposite me, and a door on my right. I was alone. I appeared to be on a sort of couch and had a blanket covering me. I did not know where I was, or what I was doing there. The door opened, and in walked a nurse. I turned to look at her, and she smiled and said, "Oh, you're awake are you, I'll go and get someone," and left before I could speak to her. I was very puzzled. I appeared to be in a hospital, but did not know why I was there. I tried to think very hard as to why I was in a hospital. Oh, of course, I thought, I am a nurse, that's why I am in a hospital. But something was wrong, in this hospital I appeared to be the patient. I tried to retrace my steps to see if I could shed any light on the matter. I remembered setting off to go to university with Tilly, perhaps that was it, we had come with the course members to look at a hospital.

I looked at my wrist and realised that in my hurry, I had forgotten my watch. I looked round the room for a clock but there wasn't one. If only I could find out the time, I would know where I was supposed to be and that might help solve the mystery. The nurse came back in at that point. "What time is it?" I asked. The nurse gave me a strange look and said "Quarter-past eight." Quarter past eight, I thought feverishly, that does not help me at all, because I should be at university. The nurse said that she would bring Tilly in to see me shortly. I was instantly relieved. Tilly would make sense of all this for me. The nurse spoke to me again, "I'll just have a look at the bandage on your head." My hands flew to my head, and there was a great turban-style bandage wrapped round my head. "Why have I got a bandage?" I asked worriedly. This was getting worse. Not only was I in a strange hospital, but the nurse was saying that I had been hurt. Why didn't I know anything about it, then? The nurse told me that I had a bandage because of the gash I had sustained in the accident. "What accident?" I gasped. The poor nurse must have really thought I'd flipped by now. "You've been in a car-crash with your friend, don't you remember?" CAR CRASH. What car crash? "No, I don't remember anything" I stammered. How could I have had a car crash and not remember? "The last thing I remember is going through the traffic lights, nothing since then." "That's right" the nurse said, "that's where the accident happened." "So where am I now?" I asked the nurse and she told me that I was in a casualty department near to where the accident had happened.

At that point Tilly arrived. Boy, was I glad to see her. Tilly came in and hugged me, and said that they had rung Jim, and Tilly's husband was bringing him over. My heart sank. I thought 'Oh no, Jim will shout first and ask questions after, he cannot cope in hospitals.' Well, it was too late, he was on his way. A doctor came in then to sew my head wound up. He explained that he would have to shave some of my hair. I said O.K. He scraped very gingerly for a few seconds and then apologised and said that he would have to shave some more. This carried on until I was beginning to think that I would have a bald head on one side. I need not have worried, it was very discreet, and I was almost able to cover it with my fringe.

Once he had stitched me up, he said he wanted to have a look at my leg. He pulled the covers away, and there under a gauze dressing was a gaping hole in my left leg, on the inside of my knee. It was really interesting, you could see all the structures, bones, fat, muscle. The doctor was telling me that I would have to go to theatre to have it sorted out, but I could not go yet, because I had been unconscious. "It is quite a serious injury" he was saying. "You will probably walk with a limp for the rest of your life." I must have still been in shock, because all I could think was that now I would have a limp like my Dad used to have. I never thought at that point that I might never walk again, or drive, or even work. The doctor left, and Tilly came back. "Oh Tilly," I said excitedly, "come and look at this hole in my leg." Tilly went pale, "No thanks," she said, "I have seen enough of it for now."

I started plying her with questions about the accident. She told me that as we went straight through the lights, a man at the filter had driven across our path. I was unconscious, and Tilly could not find a pulse and thought I was dead. Trapped in the car, she climbed out of the mini window, ran round to my side and started trying to get me out of the car to resuscitate me. At that point, two nurses arrived and took over. I have no idea who they were, apparently they just slipped away without any thanks. But I owe my life to Tilly and the two unknown helpers.

Back in the casualty department, Jim had arrived, and they brought him in to see me. I braced myself, waiting for the shouts, but all he did was take me in his arms and ask if I was all right. I was so relieved, I said "I love you." He told me later that I looked half dead, and when I said I loved him, he was convinced I was dying and making my peace with him. Oops! Eventually Tilly was allowed home but I was being kept in because I had been unconscious, and they had to sort out my knee. Tilly and Jim came in to say goodbye, and I gave Tilly a lecture about driving. "The best thing after a car crash is to get straight back in the car and drive" I said from my vast experience. Tilly just said 'yes' and they all left. She did not tell me for quite a few weeks that her brand new mini was a write-off. They never found the tin of bonfire toffee!

Meanwhile, I was taken to X-ray. As soon as I was moved from the couch I was in agony. I had not felt any pain whilst I had lain still, which was why it was difficult to believe that I had injuries. I was moved up to the surgical ward and put to bed by a nice pupil nurse who was at the end of her training. She asked if I had any pain, and when I said 'yes' she got me some paracetamols. She explained that I could not have any stronger pain killers because I had been unconscious. The pain killers did not make a scrap of difference, and I spent an agonising night. They had put a POP on my leg so that I did not bend my knee, and it was very uncomfortable and heavy. I spent the night alternately thanking God that I was alive and the other half crying in self-pity because of the pain. During one of the tearful times, the nurse caught me.

She was brilliant. She found out that I could not sleep flat on my back, so she flipped me over on my side, and I had a sleep for about half an hour. The night dragged slowly past, with the nurse coming regularly to check that I had not slipped into unconsciousness again. There is no chance of sleep when they are coming to wake you up regularly! I had a lot more empathy with head injury patients after that night! The same nurse was on for the four nights I was in that hospital, and I got to know her very well. The next day was Jim's birthday, poor lad, but he didn't get any presents. As he didn't drive in those days, he had to rely on friends and family for lifts to Manchester. At least it made Cynthia drive on a motorway. Although she had been driving for years, she avoided the motorway like the plague.

That first morning, the Sister came to talk to me, and explained that they could not take me to theatre until evening because I had been unconscious. That phrase was beginning to get on my wick. The Sister explained that I would remain without food or drink until I went to theatre. It was at this point that I became a difficult patient. "If I am not going to theatre until evening, then at least I should be able to have a drink of coffee now." The Sister gave me a long look, and then agreed. That cup of coffee was the best I have ever had. A group of doctors, pimply looking youths by and large, came by and were having a conversation about 'who wanted a go at this knee?' I sat there listening and never said a word. I had become the compliant patient again by this time.

Fortunately for me, a lady registrar came at this time, and said "Nobody will 'have a go' at this knee. This lady needs her leg for the rest of her life. We'll get the orthopaedic doctors in." I shot her a very grateful glance and the group of doctors slunk off sheepishly. The orthopaedic doctor came later, and I eventually got to theatre late that evening.

By this time Tilly had been admitted to a hospital nearer home. Whilst she had been in casualty, she would not let anyone examine her properly because she was so worried about me. It turned out that she had fractured the small bone at the top of her pelvis, which had punctured her bladder. She also had a broken wrist. And with these injuries she had climbed out of the mini window to rescue me. What a star! The staff on the ward were very good about letting us have conversations with each other to keep in touch. As Tilly had remained conscious throughout, she did not have the luxury of loss of memory like me, and had unpleasant memories for a long time. Whilst I had the phone, I managed to get through to our administrator to tell him that the competition was now ended, and anyway I had won. I had been in the local paper nine times in thirteen days, and also had an interview on Radio Lancashire about children with asthma. He gave in gracefully under the circumstances, but I never got my prize. (If you are reading this, you owe me!).

The news was getting out that Tilly and I were in hospital, and we both received many cards, flowers and visits. The doctors offered me the option of staying where I was for another three weeks to have plastic surgery, or to return nearer home. There was no contest. But then I hit bureaucracy. There were no beds. I had to stay there for three days before they found me a bed. I was transferred by a local ambulance crew who both recognised me. It was a pretty boneshaking journey. Arriving back nearer home, I was admitted to the female orthopaedic ward, and given a private cubicle because of my status. It was a boon because once the news of my return got out, I was inundated with visitors from morning to night. One visitor was the Burnley Express photographer. As he was walking through the hospital grounds, he stopped to ask directions to the ward where I was. Out of all the thousands of people there must have been in the hospital at that moment in time, he had to go and ask our adminstrator. After that, he decided that I had been involved in the car crash deliberately, to help me win the competition. I assured him that I had not!

I was visited by practically everyone I knew in the hospital. Even the Chief Nurse came to visit. One of the staff nurses also visited me with some of the children from the ward, and they brought me an enormous home-made card. I was a little worried that two of the paediatricians would play tricks on me, as they had both been in hospital and we had made them each a cheeky hospital survival kit. But they behaved impeccably, which I think was worse! On my last day, I got a visit from the local Mayor and Mayoress. They came tripping in, accompanied by their attendant who was carrying a large basket of fruit. I laughed when I saw them, but the other patients just stared. They had seen so many visitors going in and out of my cubicle that they were beginning to ask who I was. The Mayor and Mayoress just happened to be the landlord and landlady of Jim's local pub. They had been teasing him about me being in and said that they might visit me. He just thought it was a wind-up, and never said anything about it.

Tilly was on another ward but spent more time on my ward keeping me company. I was glad because I was on complete bed-rest, and Tilly was often my 'gopher.' She even had to clean me up once when I had the most appalling accident with a bed-pan. Not easy when I had a full-length POP on and Tilly's arm was in plaster. Not only my rescuer but my personal nurse as well. By this time, I had been back to theatre twice. My orthopaedic surgeon, decided that if he could pull the three ends of skin together, he would do so. Thus I would have a deformed inner knee, but I would not need a skin graft. There had been a severe infection so a skin graft would have been dodgy anyway. The graft would probably have broken down and ended up worse than before.

After a total of fifteen days in hospital, my doctor said that if I could walk up and down the stairs on crutches without weightbearing, I could go home. Boy, that was the hardest walk of my life, but there was no way that I was staying in any longer. What a relief to get home again, but mobility was very limited with not being allowed to weightbear. Jim had brought the spare bed downstairs into the living room and borrowed a Portapotti. It is very embarrassing being nursed by your own relatives, and Jim never got used to having a Portapotti in the living room! Cynthia was an excellent support during this time, as were Mum, Joe and other relatives and friends.

The week after I got home, it was the ward night out for Christmas. I decided to attend. Getting a lift up to the hairdressers, Karen blow dried my hair, very gingerly. The scar was still angry on my temple and if she asked me once if she was hurting me, she asked me a thousand times, but I never felt a thing. Still, they do say where there is no sense, there is no feeling! I dragged out an old long dress from the wardrobe to wear, so that it would cover my POP. It was then that I remembered the conversation with the colleague about having a month off work, and wearing a long dress for the night out. This was not the way I had actually intended it to be.

The plaster was removed just before Christmas. To my horror, the left leg was thin and wasted, and very hairy (something to do with the skin being covered by the plaster). I then began regular appointments at the physiotherapy department and out-patients' clinic. But I was off work a long time. My surgeon had predicted that I would be off-sick for weeks, but as time went on, the tiny fractured bones in my foot gave me a lot of pain. Eventually, after four and a half months, it was time for me to return to work. My GP reminded me that I would be on half pay if I completed more than six months sickness, so that was one incentive to go back.

I viewed the return to work with some fear and trepidation so I approached the occupational health department at the hospital about coming back to work part-time initially. I got no joy. You were either off-sick, or back full-time. I was worried because I knew that once I was back at work I would spend most of the time on my feet. You would think that in a hospital they would be more understanding, but it is not so. If anything, they are worse. If you worked in a factory, they would put you on light duties at first. But the health service is not renowned for the care it gives to the carers, although they have improved a great deal since then. Eventually, I got round it by using up my holiday entitlement that I had not used during my sickness. As it was March when I returned, I had to use my holidays up by March 31st or lose them, so I took two days holiday a week, thus making my return more gradual. This helped me tremendously, but also I sat down at every available opportunity, especially during the long ward rounds, usually taking a stool with me!

As they had managed without me for so long, it was decided to put into operation a plan that had been mooted for some time. They wanted all the sisters to rotate to the baby unit, now called NICU (neonatal intensive care unit). The idea was that once we had learnt how to use ventilators (breathing machines) on NICU we could start taking ventilated children on our ward. I was delighted. It was ten years since I had worked on the unit, and technology had moved on a pace, but I looked forward to going back, and learning lots of new skills. Once we had all been through we could then ventilate children on our own ward without them having to go to the adult Intensive Care Unit (ICU).

It had long been recognised that an adult ICU was no place for a sick child being looked after by adult nurses. But if we kept very sick children on the ward, we did not have the equipment, skills or expertise needed to nurse them anyway. A difficult dilemma. Having said that, we were lucky in that our ICU staff were excellent in caring for our children. They went out of their way to make the unit child friendly, but they did not have a lot of facilities for children and certainly no nursery nurse input. Also, some of the adult patients found it distressing to have children being nursed near them. Another compromise that was suggested was that a children's nurse would go to ICU whenever a child was admitted to advise on the paediatric side whilst the

ICU nurses did the technical stuff. In reality, we never had the spare staff for that to take place so it was a non-starter.

So in May 1985, I went back to the unit I had worked on when I was a newly qualified midwife. It was something of a culture shock when I got there. It was not only the name that had changed! (from SCBU to NICU). The basic structure was still the same - three rooms and the isolation area. The 'hot' room contained all the poorly babies. The 'warm' room contained the getting better babies. The 'cold' room had the babies who were waiting to get to a certain weight before they could be discharged home. The temperature in the 'cold' room was still roasting, so don't get any ideas that we were neglecting them. It was just that it was getting the babies more acclimatised to a home environment.

I seemed to spend the entire seven months in the 'hot' room. Usually there were one or two babies on ventilators, but that summer there seemed to be nearly always five. We had a lot of very tiny babies who had a horrendous struggle to survive at the beginning of their life. Some you thought had no chance but they pulled through. Others seemed to be progressing well then had a set back and died. You could never predict it. We had quite a bunch of regulars who were all in together. I was usually on with the same staff nurse. She was so laid back she was horizontal. We had many laughs together and many tears too, but she taught me an awful lot and kept me going. Another brilliant teacher was the senior nurse in the unit.

The worst thing about the 'hot' room was the noise. It overwhelmed me on the first day. Each baby had an incubator and several machines attached to it. There were dongs, pings and bleeps going all day long. I did not believe the staff at first when they said I would learn to differentiate between the different noises, and that after a while you only heard the worrying noises or alarms. It became almost like background music, but on that first day it terrified me. If it had that effect on me as a Sister, you can imagine the effect it had on parents who were already stressed because their baby was ill and/or premature.

A great deal of time was spent with the new parents and it certainly paid off. Very rapidly the parents adjusted to the noises and equipment and became very adept at caring for their tiny children. Some of the babies took a long time to be weaned off the ventilator on to breathing for themselves. Once they were stable, we were able to allow the parents to play with them and bath them whilst still on the ventilator. It made the parents feel that they were really involved in their child's care. Often the children were in for very long periods, even months. On occasion, the babies had a very perilous passage and we were almost praying over the incubators, especially if the baby was very precious. Whilst all babies are precious, there are some occasions when they are more precious. If the premature delivery was because of the serious ill-health of the mother, the mother may have been advised not to have any further pregnancies. If that particular baby was the first child, and would probably be the last child also, every set back caused great anxiety in both staff and parents alike. To look after these children for months on end and for them to die was very stressful.

Some of the babies got every complication going, whilst some very tiny babies sailed through with no problems at all. A great thrill on the unit was when a baby reached a hundred days old, especially if their life had been traumatic. We used to trim up the incubator and make them cards and have a bit of a party for the family. What the babies thought about it all we will probably never know!

Another thrill was to see the Mums coming to live in with their babies to get them used to looking after their babies before they were discharged home. At this time they also met the home care sister so that she could continue their care at home and support the family in the early days. It was very exciting to get a baby dressed up ready for going home. Although we were glad that progress had been made, there was a little sadness, too, as it felt as if a family member was moving away.

On the children's ward, the summer period is usually quieter, but that summer I missed out. I stayed seven months on NICU until mid-December and I never stopped. The unit was heaving for the whole seven months I was there. In mid December, I was sent back to my own ward to find myself straight into the busy bronchiolitis season. (Bronchiolitis is a viral infection that affects babies and can be very serious). It was a real baptism of fire for my return.

When I arrived back in mid-December, they asked me to go back to NICU on Christmas Eve for one afternoon to cover, as they were short staffed. I went back to find only two babies and one of them was going home. The 'hot' room was EMPTY. All the staff were sighing with relief and saying how great it was to have a quiet spell so that they could recharge their batteries. I could not believe the change in two weeks and reflected on the heaving children's ward I would return to the next day, which would probably last until Spring. Oh well, at least it kept me out of trouble.

There was a new Sister on the ward when I returned, and we worked a shift pattern out between us that worked brilliantly. We worked opposite each other and worked ten days on duty and four days off duty. It meant that whoever was on the ten day stint knew every single patient and all that was happening. On the eighth day (Wednesday) the other Sister would come back from four days off to start her ten day stint. Between Wednesday afternoon and Friday lunchtime, the reins were handed over to the other Sister.

I must just mention one regular patient and that was Cynthia's youngest, Gillian. This is not betraying patient confidentiality as I am speaking about this from an aunty's perspective. Besides, Gillian wanted a mention! She was extremely allergic to many foodstuffs and failed to thrive and had severe eczema. Her hair was thin and wispy, her skin very dry and she looked like a child from a Third World country. Her paediatrician often despaired of her as he wondered what treatment to try next. Eventually, he suggested tube-feeding Gillian with a brand new substance that was still at the experimental stages. Because it was not on general release, it hadn't got a name but was called RD156 after the laboratory's coding system. We tended to call it WD40, as that was easier to remember. Cynthia had to tube-feed Gillian regularly, even during the night. This led to disturbed sleep for Gillian, Cynthia and Peter. Often when Cynthia brought Gillian into her bed to feed her in the middle of the night, Peter would get up and go and sleep in Gillian's bed - a form of nocturnal musical beds!

One night, he was so tired that he slept throughout the whole feed. Next morning, Gillian woke and said to Cynthia, "What is Daddy doing in our bed?" However, the tube-feeding worked and Gillian started to gain weight very, very slowly, until real food could be re-introduced one by one. But it was very sad to watch her play with her dolls and tube-feed them instead of using a bottle. Her health career has lurched from crisis to crisis ever since. Her food allergies are not as severe now but she has developed asthma and nasty migraines. If she does not get the migraine treatment in soon enough, all one side of her body goes temporarily weak, like a stroke. It doesn't half frighten her teachers! Her latest stint at putting the wind up her paediatrician was on Christmas Day a couple of years ago. She was admitted to the ward completely clapped out (a very technical term meaning extremely ill) with meningococcal septicaemia. The problem was, she did not have any typical signs and symptoms, so it was only the brilliant work by her paediatrician and all the doctors and nurses that saved her life. It did, however, leave her profoundly deaf in one ear and partially deaf in the other ear. But who cares? She is alive and can still play her flute beautifully, which she did at Mum's funeral.

By the mid-eighties, the long awaited new ward started to loom on the horizon. The original plans for a new children's ward had been dropped (again) and a new state of the art surgical unit was being built. It was all red bricks and bright blue and bright green windows. The paediatricians were unhappy that the children's ward plans had been scrapped and went en masse to the hospital senior management. The result was that one of the new surgical wards was commandeered to be used as a children's ward. It was to consist of several small wards and four cubicles - twenty-one beds in all, which was less than the old ward.

We suggested several names for the new ward that sounded suitable for children, but they weren't taken up. The ward was just given a number. The plans were drawn up for a smooth transition.

CHAPTER EIGHT

A MOVING EXPERIENCE

Moving house is not an easy experience. I know, I have just done it! Moving wards is an absolute nightmare. Some of the equipment goes with you but, if you are lucky, you get quite a lot of new equipment. You are asked to make lists of what you want and then it is reduced to what you need! It then gets further reduced, usually because the building budget has gone way over. An example of this was the baby baths. On the old ward, we had baby baths built in but as the new ward had been designed as an adult ward, it had no baby baths or even small toilets either. It did have bidets however, which the children loved. They sailed boats in them, used them as small toilets (!), paddled in them, and frequently flooded them. It was not long after the move that we had them removed, I cannot remember why! The other Sister and I did not even get to look at the new ward until three weeks before the move. We were however, allowed to choose some of the equipment. We chose some very posh baby baths that incorporated wardrobe space and lots of shelves and drawers. They were very expensive. They did not order them. The only trouble was, nobody ordered any bog basic baby baths either, so we opened the ward without any!

When planning to move a children's ward, it is best to do this during the quieter season such as mid-summer when there are fewer admissions. It is also essential to ensure that there are no admissions to the unit for at least two days to allow the staff to settle in and find their feet. That is what it is best to do, but the reality was far from it. The move took place on a Saturday in December. It was the middle of the busiest season on the ward when everyone is trying to get straight and wind down for Christmas, or at least trying to take some time off.

At least the doctors promised us that all the new admissions during the weekend would go to the isolation ward. Thus we could settle in with only the patients who were too ill to go home. There was not going to be an official opening for many months until the rest of the wards were in use, but we felt that the opening of the new ward should be acknowledged. On the day before the move, our long-serving enrolled nurse was retiring, so we hit on the idea of her performing the ceremony, but knew she would not do it if we asked her.

We carefully planned the whole ceremony in absolute secrecy. The entrance to the ward was trimmed up, a ribbon fixed across the entrance and a velvet cushion found to place the scissors on. Then we hit a snag. She was left-handed or cack-handed as they say in Lancashire. As a left-hander myself, I know how difficult it is to cut with right-handed scissors. I scoured the country until I could get a pair of left-handed scissors. We got lots of the regular children and parents to come in and had them all lined up by the new ward. One of our older patients brought his trumpet to play her a solo. One of the girls was waiting with a bouquet of flowers and we had her cards and leaving present. The only problem was how to get her over there. I asked her to come with me to the new ward on some pretext. It was met with murmuring about why her, when she was never going to work in the place, but she came anyway.

I will never, ever forget the look on her face when she saw everybody. After a little speech, the trumpet solo, the flowers, and the photos, she took the scissors in her left-hand . . . . .and promptly swapped them over to her right hand! Humph! "I have been all over for those left-handed scissors for you," I whinged. She laughed as she cut the ribbon and said that after years of trying to use scissors with her left hand, she had given up and swopped to her right.

The planning for the move had to be carried out in minute detail. As many patients as possible were sent home and the staff divided into two teams. The 'before' team were on the late shift and the 'after team' were on the early shift. We had been allowed into the ward only the day before the move. During that day all the staff had walked over to the ward with bits of equipment that they thought we would not need. They tried to familiarise themselves with the new layout, have a look in the cupboards and work out how the emergency buzzers worked. After I had finished work, I went home, collected Jim, and went back to the ward to finish putting things away. It was quite eerie at night as we were the first ward to open, and there were no other lights on, hence going for Jim!

Next morning, the ward aide and I arrived early to finish off last minute preparations. The move was planned for one o'clock.

At one, the 'before' team arrived on the late shift, had a report on each patient, then walked across to the new ward to get there 'before' the patients arrived. The 'after' team stayed behind with the children to ensure continuity as the children had got used to those members of staff during the morning. Lists were drawn up by the 'after' team of which children would go in which ambulance and with which nurse. The poorliest children were left until last so that all the other children were settled before the poorly ones came across.

The whole of the transfer went like a military operation and we were very pleased at the smooth transition. We had just got the last of the children transferred over when the phone rang. It made me jump as I was unused to the new tones. I had to think carefully before I answered. We now had a new ward number. It was the switchboard operator. "Oh hello Sister," she said, " are you settled in OK?" How nice of her to ring, I thought to myself. I should have known better. "Yes," I replied, "we are nicely settled in, thanks." "Oh good," she said, "there is an ambulance waiting to bring an admission for you." "Whoa, not so fast," I gasped, "there has been a mistake, all the emergency admissions are going to the isolation ward this weekend." "Yes, I know," replied the operator, "but the doctor says that this one is too poorly to go up to the other ward because it is too far away." I tried arguing to no avail and my first new admission arrived virtually at the same time as the other patients. So much for the fine promise of no admissions. I was on the 'before' team on the late shift. I had worn my dungarees and tee-shirt in the morning and never got round to getting changed into my uniform. By the end of the shift I stuck a label on myself saying 'Sister' because it was a little confusing for the families. The staff all worked like Trojans, especially some of the staff who had come in on their day off. I do not think anyone had any problems sleeping that night, we were all shattered.

The official opening took place eventually and the honour went to Tony Newton, who was the Minister for Health. One of the paediatricians and I showed him round the ward and as he was leaving, he turned to me and said, "You run a happy ship here, Sister." It was a proud moment for me. I always liked to think the ward was happy. It was disorganised, chaotic, crazy, mad, hard-work but usually happy. I often had all the day's paperwork piled up on my desk as I started the next job without having finished the last job. A piled up desk became known as a 'Linda' desk (and still is to this day). 'E' was one of the night staff and I nearly drove her to distraction. To say that 'E' was tidy was a slight understatement. Did I say slight? Words like fanatical, obsessive, pernickety spring to mind. She often did a night shift when I was on a late shift and used to come upstairs asking "is Linda on duty?" and groaning when the answer was yes. Her pet phrase was, "one of these days I am going to come on days and sort you out, lady." But we never quite managed it. As she rotated onto days, I went onto nights. We were very fortunate that we had our own night staff who only worked on our ward and they were all very experienced. This had built up over the years as a lot of the other night staff declined to come on the children's ward because they did not like it. Eventually with rotation, all our night staff came on days.

We soon settled into our surroundings. There was an outdoor playground which was very posh but obviously designed by a childless person (probably a man as well). The fence surrounding the outdoor play area consisted of sawn logs driven into the ground, that were a foot to eighteen inches high, so even the smallest toddler could 'escape'. It was difficult for the playstaff to work in. It also had a beautiful glass dome structure that housed a sand pit. The children loved it. One little boy wrote me a letter. First of all, he thanked all the doctors and nurses for making him better. (I think his Mum had dictated that bit.) He then said that he liked being in hospital because we had a sand pit. Unfortunately, the local hooligans liked it too and eventually it had to be pulled down. The glass was always being broken into the sand and it became a serious health hazard.

The following year brought new changes to the ward when the children's surgical ward from the other hospital moved in next door. This was great for us because if we had an admission that needed an operation, we used to have to move them to the other hospital. This took time and effort, not to mention an ambulance and its crew. Now we could just take the child and family next door ourselves and keep in contact with them as the child recovered from surgery. The ward was run by a Sister who had worked with us as a staff nurse before going to the surgical ward. We worked very closely together and it was much better to have all the children together in the same hospital. The surgical ward was staffed by doctors who cared primarily for adults but also operated on children. They were not trained paediatricians. Some of them were not as good at talking to children and parents which was so different from our ward where doctors constantly talked to parents and children.

Our doctors had stopped wearing white coats years before so that they did not frighten the children, but the surgeons still wore theirs. Some of the older surgeons were quite pompous and very old school. Whereas we only had three paediatricians initially, the surgical ward had many consultant surgeons to deal with. Besides them, there were all the registrars, senior house officers, house officers and even a medical student or two. Not all of the surgeons were pompous. Some were the very opposite and had great fun with the children. The urologist was one of these. I always remember one little circumcised toddler holding his nappy away from his penis saying, "Ooh, hurt," very loudly when the urologist came to visit. The urologist just stood by the cot with bowed head and apologised to the child for hurting him. All his patients loved him - except, perhaps, for those who were having circumcisions!

We soon became used to having the surgical ward next door and being able to help each other out during busy spells. There was far less isolation than there had been for the staff previously. The following year brought more changes as an extension was built onto the main ward. This consisted of cubicles and was attached on to the main corridor of the ward. The suggestion was that the new part of the ward had the suffix 'A' added to the end of the main wards' name. We felt that was an awful title. It did not give the isolation ward staff a real identity as they would just feel like an extension of the main ward. We suggested the ward should be named after the first paediatrician, but the hospital planners were not too keen as all the other wards in the hospital had numbers. I don't know how we won this one, but win we did, and it was named after the paediatrician. It was duly opened by him and he was delighted, as most people wait to commemorate you until after you are dead!

The new layout of the ward meant that you had to walk several extra miles a day because you could not see all the patients at the same time. On the old ward we were understaffed according to national guidelines for a 'nightingale' ward and it was acknowledged that a ward with cubicles and bays needed more staff. Did I get any? I did not. This became a perennial issue as internal markets started being introduced into the NHS. Money became the prime motivator for action instead of patient needs. It's all right saying that you can perform so many hip operations per week, but on a medical ward things are not always so straightforward. A visit to hospital for pneumonia may only require two days stay, but then again, it may be two months. Unfortunately, the diseases don't yet know that they are supposed to comply with the stated length of stay so that the cost of the admission keeps to the predicted hospital budget. Perhaps in the future with genetic engineering . . . . .

I began to get more and more fed up with the demands made by the bureaucracy and the constant staff shortages. If a member of staff went off-sick, you could spend nearly all day on the phone trying to sort out a replacement. You had a number of people who were on the bank and prepared to come in at short notice to help out. Nowadays, most hospitals have a bank co-ordinator who takes all the tedious administration away from the Sister. Also, budgets that were once held solely by the managers were coming down to ward level, and Sisters were supposed to add budgeting to their list of manifold skills. The advantage was that you had more autonomy over the ward area. However, if you had a run where a lot of staff were off-sick, the budget went through the roof, through no fault of your own. Equipment started being delivered from the stores with the price per unit printed on. This was no bad thing, as it prevented needless waste. But all these new skills took time away from the patients, parents, and students who were allocated to the ward to learn about children's nursing.

As the senior nurse, I should have been giving the best care to the children. In reality the care was very fragmented because I was always being called away to a meeting or to answer a query on the phone. Or I would be stuck on yet another ward round when the child's care was due. Eventually, I gave up allocating myself any patients. The system is much better nowadays. The doctor visits each patient with the 'named nurse' who is looking after the patient for the day. With this method, they have a lot better idea of how the child is, than a Sister who is trying to remember everyone. Not all places are doing this as some doctors still prefer the Sister to attend the ward rounds, but they are so time-consuming.

The most annoying thing would be when you were called to the phone. You broke off the conversation or task you were undertaking, walked all the way back to the nurse's station to the phone. The laboratory staff would tell you that a blood specimen you had sent was clotted and they needed a repeat specimen. Now why on earth could they have not told the ward aide that message? Actually they would have had a better chance of getting action if they told her rather than me because I have an atrocious memory. But no, they always had to speak directly to Sister. It was one of my pet hates. Teaching the students was always a real joy for me, but again I found I was teaching them less and less and this increased my dissatisfaction.

As I started to look at my long term prospects, a teaching career seemed more and more attractive. This would still involve children's nursing but would give me the opportunity to develop my teaching skills. Knowing that nursing was moving towards becoming a graduate profession, it seemed sensible to work towards a degree myself. Over the last few years I had done many courses and was now at diploma level, so it was a natural progression to go for a part-time degree. A new degree had just commenced from what was then the Lancashire Polytechnic. You could do the first year subjects at a local college and only move to Preston for later study. This seemed like a good idea, as I could see if I could cope with the work before committing myself to the whole degree. With the ultimate plan of being a nurse tutor, I took the subject of Education Studies. It was a very good course. Towards the end of the course we found out that some of us could have had exemption for the first year because of our teaching certificates. The group was again made up largely of nurses along with a tax inspector, an engineer and a headteacher.

The members of the group supported each other very well and most of us went on to Preston to complete our degrees, some on a full-time basis and some on a very part-time basis. Because I already had a diploma, I was able to get some more exemptions, but it still took me four years on a part-time basis. After a long chat with my boss she suggested that I go on to night duty for a month. It would give me a break as the bureaucracy was really getting to me and I felt that I needed a change. It was the best thing that I had done for a long time. Nights were bliss. It was no easier work, but the peace was indescribable. If I started doing a job, I could finish it, which was pretty novel. I actually took an active part in nursing care that I had been doing less and less of on days. And the phone hardly ever rang, or if it did, it was a legitimate use of my time. I even had time to teach, although with the most interested audience and the best will in the world, learning new facts is difficult at 4 am!

When I started on nights I only did part-time which was three nights a week. It was enough, as during this time I was attending the Poly one or two days a week. Added to that, my stepfather, Joe was dying from lymphoma, and Mum had a nervous breakdown because she could not cope. Three months after Joe died, my stepbrother Rex, found out he was dying from mesothelioma. Rex survived his Dad by ten months, leaving behind a very young widow and a lovely six months old baby girl, Rachel. This was hardly an atmosphere conducive to academic study. But I kept going, mainly because of the superb support of the night staff. They swapped off-duty for me. The other night sister worked split nights so that I could go to the Poly for my lessons. Only once did I have to go straight to Poly from night-duty but it was a waste of time. I was fine until eleven o'clock, but I don't remember a thing after that.

I knew that if I could complete my degree, I would have a better chance of obtaining a post in teaching. Other staff nurses and enrolled nurses helped me with my assignments or fed babies for me so that I could study if the ward was quiet. 'F' was one of the night staff who took it upon herself to sort me out. (I think 'E' had given her the challenge). We hit it off on the wrong note initially but we soon sorted it out and became firm allies. She said my untidiness was diabolical and taught me how to keep the desk a lot tidier. I responded well to my mentor's teaching and she was well pleased with my progress. The auxiliary nurses on nights were all brilliant, too. They had all worked on children's wards for years. They could have run the ward blindfolded, with one hand behind their backs. Well, actually, they did run the ward but were kind enough to let us think we were in charge. The month that the boss suggested that I spend on nights stretched into three years and they were very happy ones for me, apart from the family tragedies.

I think one of the sweetest moments of the whole three years (nay, my whole career) was coming on night duty one night when 'E' was on the late shift and the ward was like a pigsty.

Oh, what bliss, what justice, what happiness, what joy, as 'E' apologised to ME for not being ready for handover and the ward being untidy. In a small voice she admitted that she had had no idea when she was on night duty how difficult it could be on days. It took a long time for me to wipe the big smile off my face. Miss Perfection had slipped ever so slightly, but I must stress, that was only on one occasion. Every other time she was spot on with the tidiness.

In the school of nursing there were about eight tutors and between them they had worked in most of the specialities that were taught in the curriculum. All that is, except for paediatrics. Usually they conned one of the tutors to teach paediatrics but she often felt inadequate because she had not undergone children's nurse training. She was our ward link tutor who helped us support the students through their paediatric experience. As I was keen to use my newly learnt teaching skills, I told her that I would be quite happy to come and be a guest speaker to teach paediatrics. She was delighted and I was soon a regular visitor to the school. It also meant that I had got my foot in the door and was increasing my experience and abilities as a teacher.

The exciting day came when the director sent for me because he had decided he needed a paediatric tutor. He explained that he had not got a vacancy just then. He said that if I was prepared to go on a full-time tutor's course for nine months, he would second me. He would also ask my boss to keep my job open in case he had not got a vacancy at the end of the teaching course. I was a bit sceptical at this but, lo and behold, my boss agreed and even confirmed it in writing. (I made about four copies of the letter in case I lost one!) I was ecstatic until he told me that before he was prepared to sponsor me, he wanted to listen to me teaching. We duly got our diaries together and the only session we could both attend was on intestinal obstruction. Me, who had never worked in surgery since qualifying. With a confident smile, I agreed and then ran home and panicked. 'Well,' I rationalised, 'if I can teach that, I can teach anything.' After the lecture he gave his verdict and said he was prepared to sponsor me. Phew! But he brought me down to earth with a bump by saying that next time I taught, he suggested that I put my acetate on the overhead projector the right way round! Shortly after this trial by acetate he rang me to say that he was advertising a position. Only two of us applied, myself and a lady from another hospital who was already teaching. My heart sunk, as I was sure she would get the job. Apparently it was very close but I managed to get the job and prepared to start a new era in my life.

Having only three weeks left of my degree course certainly helped me to get the job, plus the fact that I had been teaching at the local technical college on the BTec nursery nurse course.

Before I started my new job, the staff organised a leaving 'do' for me but I had to complete my final night duty first. It was all quiet on the ward when we arrived on duty. One of the auxiliaries and I were on together and we sorted the children out before we settled the ward down for the night. At ten to ten, the phone rang. It was to tell us that a very poorly baby was coming in. It was action stations all night after that as we ran round to deal with the baby. By morning we were exhausted and had not even had time to party in our lunch break ("what lunch break?" I hear the auxiliary asking). As I had been concentrating on the baby, the paperwork had been left. The papers on the desk were piled high in gay abandon. I left as I had started, with a 'Linda' desk! I didn't half get a lot of fly comments that morning.

The leaving party started well with lots of goodies and visitors, both off-duty staff and regular patients joining the staff on duty. One of the regular families brought me a picture of their children as a leaving present. Things like these are so precious and I shall treasure it for the rest of my life. In fact, the photo takes pride of place on my window sill at work. One of the doctors arrived a little later than the others and brought a lovely trifle to add to the goodies. I don't know what gave me that sixth sense but I swerved away suddenly and got the 'trifle' in my hair instead of my face. It had been made of shaving foam. What a mess I looked. I had been to the hairdressers prior to the party and had been looking pretty swish, but I looked like a disaster area now.

I berated the doctor, laughing and giving most of the shaving foam back, when one of the staff said it was not fair as I had not got the real culprit. I stopped and looked amazed. "Well whose idea was it then?" I asked. It turned out to be the idea of the paediatrician that I had April Fooled on his first day, but he had chickened out of actually doing it. He arrived shortly afterwards and I probably would not have retaliated but he walked on the ward with a smirk on his face. That did it. I scraped copious amounts of the shaving foam off my hair and wiped it on his. The look of shock on his face was a treat. I asked him afterwards why he had planned it and he simply answered "well, you April Fooled me when I first started." I looked back with disbelief. "But that was eleven years ago," I replied. I am glad I never did anything to really upset him!

The presents then started arriving from the staff and included a massive leather handbag (I still had the fetish), a gold necklace, flowers and a massive card that everyone had signed. I also received presents from individual members of staff. All in all, it was a very moving (not to mention foaming) experience. As I left the ward, my thoughts were very much on the brilliant friends I had and how much I would miss them, and the children and families. I only hoped my new career would give me as much friendship and job satisfaction as the last twelve years had on the children's ward. I got in the car and slowly drove away, back to the hairdressers - well you didn't think I was going to go home looking like that, did you? I do have some pride.